REVOLUTIONARIES

[The WORLD TURNED UPSIDE DOWN]

JOSHUA GAY

HIGH PRAISE MEDIA

Parsons Publishing House
Your Voice Your World™

Revolutionaries: The World Turned Upside Down.
by Joshua Gay

Parsons Publishing House
Christiansburg, VA 24073 USA
www.ParsonsPublishingHouse.com
Info@ParsonsPublishingHouse.com

Publisher's Note: Publisher has opted to reference satan and related names with lowercase letters.

Cover Art: Micah Gay

ISBN-13: 978-1602730946
ISBN-10: 1602730946
Library of Congress Control Number: 2017909193
Printed in the United States of America.
For World-Wide Distribution.

WHAT PEOPLE ARE SAYING...

In his book, ***Revolutionaries: The World Turned Upside Down***, Pastor Joshua Gay lays out emphatically what the role of the Church is in this critical time. A revelation that comes straight from the throne room of God. This book has the potential to change a culture. Read it, spread it, and by all means, activate it!—**Pastor Judy Jacobs,** Dwelling Place Church International, Cleveland TN, Author & Worship Leader

Pastor Joshua Gay has clearly heard a word from God and has captured it in this book to share with us. He begins with a revelatory dream that demonstrates with great force God's plan for cultural transformation. Then, Pastor Joshua blends Scripture and history to teach us what revolutionaries in action look like. On these pages, you'll find a fresh call to engage and change your world. This book will compel you to dream about revolution, envisioning what "sudden change" can look like through your life. —**Micah Wood**, Director, The RAMP School of Ministry, Hamilton AL

It is no surprise to me that Joshua Gay has been chosen by God to release this revelation of revival, reformation, and sonship. I have seen him live this message out and know you will be blessed by the identity it will bring in your own life.—**Karen Wheaton,** Founder & Senior Leader, The Ramp

In his book, ***Revolutionaries***, Joshua Gay stirs the heart of the reader to rise up and become a world changer and a freedom maker. As we engage in the fray, young and old together can be formed as a company of people who turn the world upside down! It is our day! Get in the fight! —**Pastor Jane Hamon,** Vision Church, Santa Rosa Beach FL, Author

In this book, Joshua Gay has masterfully woven biblical revelation with historical facts and released a new, BOLD challenge for Revolutionaries to arise and turn this world upside down and inside out for the kingdom of God!—**Pastor David Reddick,** Christ Family Church, Crestview FL

This book is a voice to our generation that resonates what God is saying to the Christian believer today. Pastor Joshua's words will challenge your walk with God and encourage you with practical ways to live a revolutionary life. —**Pastor Herber Lopez,** Iglesia Cielos Abiertos, Gainesville GA

Joshua Gay has clearly charted a roadmap that guides us back to the purposes of the Father, and it can only be navigated by a remnant group of revolutionaries. I am certain you will sense the flames of revolution begin to stir afresh in your own heart as the revelation in the following pages awaken you to your mantle and mandate. Let the revolution BEGIN! —**PASTOR CASEY DOSS,** HOPE UNLIMITED CHURCH, KNOXVILLE TN

In his new book, ***Revolutionaries: The World Turned Upside Down***, Joshua Gay reveals that there is a new generation rising—armed with the history of the past, but also with a new fire and direction for what is to come in the church's future. I highly recommend this prophetic book. —**PASTOR KEN BLOUNT,** KEN BLOUNT MINISTRIES, OKLAHOMA CITY OK

To appreciate real change, one must be driven to bring the change that matters. Joshua Gay empowers this reality in ***Revolutionaries: The World Turned Upside Down***. If you are passionate about changing the world for Christ, you will discover yourself in this RIGHT NOW book. POWERFUL!—**PASTOR JAMIE TUTTLE,** DWELLING PLACE CHURCH INTERNATIONAL, CLEVELAND TN

If you are looking for a book that will usher you into the supernatural purpose of God—this is it! Joshua Gay has a passion and a purity that brings force and clarity to release a double portion anointing. ***Revolutionaries*** contains the heart of God, prophetically igniting everything it touches! —**PASTOR KENNY MECKFESSEL,** NEW LIFE CHURCH, SHERWOOD AR

Pastor Joshua Gay has brilliantly written a revealing and challenging word for the body of Christ to recognize the urgency of our hour that is upon us. ***Revolutionaries*** is a call to this generation to recognize the importance of being the type of leader who refuses to allow the culture of today to direct the understanding of God's Word. You are not only a world changer, but a revolutionary!—**RYAN JOHNSON,** RYAN JOHNSON MIN., FORT PAYNE AL

As Christians, Jesus commanded and equipped us to effect lasting transformation in ourselves and the world in which we live. In ***Revolutionaries***, Joshua Gay presents fresh, inspiring, and practical revelation to do just that through biblical and historical teachings. —**PASTOR CHRIS GABRIELSON**, HIGH PRAISE CENTRAL MINNESOTA, ST. CLOUD MN

Every page of this book will stir you to become a revolutionary for the kingdom of God.—**JOE JOE DAWSON,** BURN TEXARKANA, TEXARKANA TX, AUTHOR, FOUNDER OF ROAR APOSTOLIC NETWORK

ACKNOWLEDGMENTS

I would like to recognize and thank all the wonderful people who have been such a blessing during the process of writing this book.

First, I want to thank my wife, Miranda. You are my best friend, greatest encourager, and the person I love the most in this world. Your words and actions continue to encourage me to pursue everything that God has called us to accomplish. Thank you for continually being there to listen to me, to support me, and to help in any way that you can. You are a rock that I know is always there for me. Your love, compassion, and willingness to put the Lord first in everything is an inspiration to me and so many others. I look forward to continuing to serve Jesus and His Church together for the rest of our lives. I love you.

I also want to thank my three children: Josiah, Hannalee, and Eliza. There are not enough words in the world to describe how proud Daddy is of you three. Your love for Jesus and the moving of the Lord is so obvious at even a young age. I know that God has great plans for your lives. I am blessed that our Heavenly Father entrusted your mother and I with the privilege of stewarding your lives. Daddy loves you.

I want to recognize my parents, Robert and Stacey Gay. You have been and continue to be such an incredible example of a godly marriage and ministers who walk in integrity. I can never thank you enough for being biblical parents who raised me in the fear and admonition of the Lord. You recognized the gifts and callings on my life and put a demand on what the Lord placed inside of me. Thank for continuing to encourage me to this very day. I love you both so much.

I would like to acknowledge my siblings, Micah Gay and Kayla Hill, and their spouses, Chelsea Gay and Kelvin Hill. I love you all deeply. Your friendship and encouragement are an invaluable part of my life. Miranda and I love and appreciate you guys so much.

I want to acknowledge our High Praise family. I frequently say that a church is nothing if not a family; I am blessed to have such a large, encouraging, and anointed family. I specifically want to thank the High Praise Orlando church family. In May of 2015, we embarked on a journey of planting a church in the Central Florida area. We had no idea what was going to happen, but we knew that God called us, and so we obeyed and went. Little did I know how much God was going to bless us by sending us some of the most incredible people I've ever met to link up with the vision God placed within us. In my wildest dreams, I never imagined the incredible quality of people God would bring to High Praise Orlando. Thank you for every word of encouragement you gave me during the process of writing this book. Thank you for being so incredibly supportive of what God is doing at High Praise Orlando. Thank you so much; I love you all.

FOREWORD

DR. BILL HAMON
FOUNDER, CHRISTIAN INTERNATIONAL MINISTRIES

This book is very timely for the body of Christ, the Church. But beware, if you read this book you are going to be enlightened, motivated and activated into being one of God's "Revolutionaries." As you read this book you will sense the author's passion and conviction concerning the challenging truths being presented. Though Joshua is a young married minister with three children, he is not a novice concerning biblical truth and spiritual ministry.

I have known Joshua Gay since he was two years old. At that time his father, Apostle Robert Gay, was serving as a key staff member of Christian International. Joshua is now pastoring a church he helped his father plant in Orlando, Florida. Joshua is demonstrating more present truth and revelation of God's purpose for His Church than most ministers twice his age and years of ministry.

The main message of this book proclaims that God is raising up a generation of revolutionaries that will turn this world upside down like the First-Generation Church did. At the present, the world seemingly has the upper hand and is on the "upside." But God's revolutionaries will "turn the world upside down" and will cause the Church-Kingdom to be on the "upside." Let me assure you that the truths presented are not just the zealous thoughts of an over active imagination of a young minister. For myself and numerous other apostles and prophets are seeing the same thing, though we may use different terms to describe the same purpose God is seeking to fulfill.

Personally, I am 83 years of age and have been an ordained minister for 63 years and am still passionate and zealous for what God has purposed for the Omega generation to fulfill before Jesus returns to earth.

In the 1980's, I received the revelation of the company of prophets that God was raising up and pioneered the Prophetic Movement. The company of prophets was to prepare the way and make ready a prophetic people to reveal and fulfill all the prophetic Scriptures that must be fulfilled before the second coming of Jesus can take place.

In 2008, God revealed that the "Third and Final Church Reformation" was being decreed from heaven and birthed in the Church. I then wrote the book to reveal what was to be fulfilled during the Third Reformation.

In 2016, God revealed that He was activating His army into actively aggressive offensive Warriors. I then wrote the book, ***God's World War III*** to describe how the Saint's Army can and will win the war. Each term we use to describe this final purpose of God shows a different aspect of God's special people for this end-time purpose of God. The terms Kingdom Influencers, Omega Generation, God's 3rd Reformation Reformers, World War III Warriors or Revolutionaries are the same group of saints seen and described from different angles.

Let me assure you that the truths presented in this book are scriptural and dear to the heart of Jesus. These special saints will not stop until the glory of the Lord covers the earth as the waters cover the sea and the kingdoms of this world have become the kingdom of our Lord Jesus and His *Ekklesia*—His governmental body on earth.

Joshua, I am proud to be your Papa-Bishop. I pray that all my natural and spiritual children and grandchildren will have God's passion and vision for this generation as you have. I want them to have the zeal, conviction, and dedication you have in your life and ministry as revealed in this book. You are a fulfillment of a proclamation I have made often concerning my natural and spiritual sons and daughters: "I expect you to do twice as much as I do in my lifetime, but you will not win by default for I am never going to stop running this race. You just have to run until you catch me and pass me." Joshua, you are running and I am confident and praying for it to be so, that you will keep running until you pass this ole forerunner and raise up the revolutionaries that will turn this world upside down, fulfill all prophetic Scriptures, and prepare the way for the return of our Lord and Savior Jesus Christ.

Dr. Bill Hamon
Bishop, Christian International Apostolic & Global Network
Santa Rosa Beach, Florida

TABLE OF CONTENTS

"THESE WHO HAVE TURNED THE WORLD UPSIDE DOWN HAVE COME HERE TOO..."

[ACTS 17:6]

PREFACE

> We hold these truths to be self-evident, that all men are created equal, that they are endowed by their Creator with certain unalienable Rights, that among these are Life, Liberty and the pursuit of Happiness.
>
> —The Declaration of Independence

The Declaration of Independence, the document that began a process of revolution in the American colonies, commenced with a statement that detailed the essential reason for the coming Revolutionary War. What were these reasons? Thomas Jefferson outlined them: life, liberty, and the pursuit of happiness. These ideals build upon each other. These three ideals are a succinct purpose for America seeking freedom in the eighteenth century. These are still the same purposes for revolution today. Life and liberty being released are the goal of spiritual revolution.

If any revolutionary movement is for anything other than releasing life and liberty, it is nothing more than a rebellion. While rebellion unequivocally is not from God, revolution is. At times people confuse the two because they can look similar in operation. However, the difference is the intended purpose and fruit that is produced subsequently. Life is released through revolution, while bondage and destruction are released through rebellion. In August of 1861, The New York Times published an article that contrasted rebellion and revolution. The following is what was written:

> Another point of difference between rebellion and revolution is that while rebellions are generally wrong, revolutions are always right. A rebellion, as has been shown by a modern philosophic historian, is too often the mad and passionate effort of ignorant persons, who are impatient under some immediate injury, and never stop to investigate its remote and general causes. But a revolution...is a splendid and imposing spectacle, because to the moral quality of indignation produced by the presence of evil, it adds the intellectual qualities of foresight and combination; and uniting in the same act some of the highest properties of our nature, it achieves the double purpose, not only punishing the oppressor, but also relieving the oppressed.

As you begin to read this book, we must not confuse the idea of rebellion and revolution. That is imperative. In this age, God is not approving rebellious combatants with no purpose. Rather, His Spirit is empowering Holy Ghost Revolutionaries who are bringing freedom and liberty to the captives. The spirit of godly revolution is bringing true happiness (prosperity, thriving, and success) that Jefferson wrote of in the Declaration of Independence. Warriors are being released to punish the oppressor (the enemy and his minions) and relieve the oppressed (those still living in sin and those living below God's best for their lives). The revolution that is being heralded in this book isn't against any person, denomination, church, government, or political system. This revolution wages war against our enemy named satan.

We can learn so much as we traverse through history and observe the behaviors of those who have preceded us. This book is more than a recounting of history, but we will look to the American Revolution and many other great figures who lived a revolutionary life. Why? It is because I believe these people mirrored characteristics in the natural that God is causing to be released in the lives of those who are being called as revolutionaries.

God consistently used things in the natural to reveal spiritual principles. Jesus constantly preached using parables. As Jesus told these stories, He used natural principles to bring to life kingdom realities to those who were listening. Continuing in this pattern, John would use the natural maturation process to show us the process of spiritual maturity in his letters (1 John 2:12-14). There is a mirroring between the natural and spiritual. We see many spiritual principles that are mirrored in the natural realm. Throughout this book, we will be looking at many historical figures and accounts as we begin to draw spiritual principles from these narratives.

In recent history, there has been a groaning in the earth for revolution that I have observed. As a student of history, one need look no further than the 2016 Presidential election cycle in the United States to see this phenomenon. Bernie Sanders, a United States Senator from Vermont who ran for President on the Democratic platform, used the campaign slogan "A Political Revolution Is Coming." Meanwhile, Donald Trump, the man who would eventually win the 2016 Presidential election, was considered the "outsider" by both the media and the populous. Many viewed both these men as revolutionary figures. They stood promising that things would be done differently than the way they had ever been done previously if elected as President. They were promising to bring an end to the status quo. They promised a revolution that would be brought to Washington. The idea of revolution resonated in both political parties in America during the 2016 election.

Continuing in the revolutionary trend, in Europe we saw the "Brexit." This vote began a process by which the United Kingdom began to withdraw from the European Union. This was a revolutionary move as people in the United Kingdom became tired of the status quo. The political climate has been rapidly and radically changing.

It cannot be ignored that people are desirous of revolution in this day and hour. This is no coincidence. The very idea of revolution has been on the minds of many in this hour. Why? I believe it is because revolution is on the heart and agenda of heaven.

When God prepares to release something in the earth, the heart of man begins to long for the upcoming spiritual season. At times men will attempt to accomplish through natural means what God wants to accomplish through the work of the Holy Spirit. We must be cautious in a time where we sense God is stirring revolution that we refrain from attempting to fulfill it through our own strength. There was a reason that God told Zerubbabel, "'Not by might nor by power, but by My Spirit,' says the Lord of hosts." (Zechariah 4:6) What He is calling us to do isn't through what we can do, but rather what He can do.

It is equally important to understand that revolution will not be accomplished due to our strength or lack of it. The idea of bringing about a revolution in society today can be daunting. We look and see the mounting tide of immorality and feel insufficient. Remember, it isn't about you, but about His power that works through you. His power is a revolutionary power that is destined to bring life and liberty.

What we observe man desiring in the natural is merely a reflection of a hunger for what God is preparing to do in the spirit realm. What we see throughout history are characteristics that we as spiritual revolutionaries should possess. We are on the verge of the greatest spiritual revolution the world has ever seen. We are on the precipice of seeing bondages broken and freedom being released on a level unlike anything we have ever experienced in our time. Revolution is coming to turn the world upside down and bring freedom in this hour.

Join me on the journey of the revolutionary and learn how you can be one He is calling forth in this hour to turn the world upside down!

CHAPTER 1

THE DREAM

Be faithful. Receive the double portion. Change the world.

These were the last three sentences and statements that I wrote in my book ***Sonship: The Mantle. The Journey. The Double Portion.*** A strong prophetic declaration and charge was given to a generation who would be willing to walk the road of sonship and receive a double portion mantle and anointing. Those who embrace the path of sonship are destined to be world-changers.

I remember my elation as those last keys were struck on my laptop. Tears filled my eyes because of the sensation of completion and satisfaction I felt in that moment. My journey of writing the book the Lord placed within my heart had been completed. After many days and nights spent sitting at a desk and on my couch in front of a computer typing hours upon end, there was a completed book. Praise God! My heart was full of joy and so my work was completed. Or so I thought. Little did I know that God wasn't finished with this assignment just yet.

After the completion of my writing, editing of the book, and the printing process, I traveled to Atlanta, Georgia. On June

23, 2014 in Atlanta, I participated in a large Christian publishing trade show where I sat in a convention center and signed hundreds of copies of ***Sonship: The Mantle. The Journey. The Double Portion.*** It would be dishonest if I said that this wasn't an exhilarating experience for me. I had witnessed my father writing numerous books. Many great men of God had spoken into my life concerning writing books, also. Finally, I had accomplished and fulfilled a portion of the destiny over my life. I was full. I was satisfied.

Not only had I written a book of which I was pleased, but had also released a revelation that God had imparted to me that was to be propagated in the Church. It was an understanding of a double portion generation that God desires to raise up in the earth today through the biblical pattern of spiritual sons (daughters) and spiritual fathers (mothers). To this very day, I believe with everything inside me that God is raising up a generation who are submitted to spiritual authority. Moreover, I believe their lifestyles of submission and obedience properly position them to receive a double portion birthright inheritance of anointing, power, and influence that can only come from heaven above.

I believe a double portion generation will move in signs, wonders, and miracles. I believe a double portion generation will boldly declare the Word of God. I believe those who choose to embrace the biblical pattern of sonship and receive a double portion mantle are called to be history makers and world shakers. However, their ministry must consist of more than just a spiritual calling and some catchy buzzwords. Why are they called? What is the ultimate purpose of their miraculous works? Why must a double portion generation arise in the earth today?

The Question

Let's trace back for a moment to the Christian book convention in Atlanta where I attended. The night of the book signing, I returned to my hotel room. Once my family had gone to sleep, the Lord asked me a question. Now, this was nothing new to me. Frequently, when God speaks to me it is in the form a question, especially when He wants me to give deep thought and contemplation to a subject. The question He asked me was intriguing and challenging. As clear as anyone speaking to me in the natural, I heard this; "For what purpose is a double portion generation being raised up?"

Suddenly, all the feeling of completion and accomplishment I previously possessed over the achievement of my book began to fade away. Why did the swagger and elation begin to subside? The answer was quite simple: I had no clear and concise answer to the question God posed to me.

I had written thousands of words about a double portion generation. Yet, I had no answer for the question God asked me. Franticly searching for an appropriate response, I attempted to answer in the most religious and ambiguous manner that I could. I said, "Father, they are being raised up for Your purposes." I assumed that my answer was vague and broad enough to be accepted. I was wrong.

Once again, God asked me the question, "For what purpose is a double portion generation being raised up?" By the fact that God had raised this query once again, it was very clear to me that my answer was insufficient. This time I didn't even bother to attempt a response. I felt deflated and defeated. I felt as if my assignment was incomplete.

The question continued to resonate inside my mind and spirit over the course of the next day. It was a thought and question that I could not escape. Every time I tried to shift my thought process, God again asked the question, "For what purpose is a double portion generation being raised up?" At times, it was almost agitating. It was not merely because of the question being posed to me. The issue that was upsetting and getting under my skin was the fact that I had no substantive answer for the question.

Little did I know that God was setting me up to reveal the answer and bring greater understanding. Realize, God doesn't ask you a question to simply ask a question. Our Father asks a question because He wants to reveal something significant to us. This question was preparing me for one of the most significant encounters of my life to date. That encounter took place within a dream.

The Dream

After being asked the same question repeatedly throughout the course of the day, night fell and it was time to turn in and sleep. I was hoping a good night's rest and the dawning of a new day would alleviate me from thinking on the question God had repetitively asked me.

On that summer night in June in the greater Atlanta metro area, I had a vivid dream. Although I rarely remember my dreams, it was different this night. I remembered every detail of this prophetic dream. This dream was one that would begin to shape what I viewed concerning what and who God is raising up in this hour. This dream is the foundational reason that I am writing this today. Let me share with you what God showed me in that dream.

In my dream, I was brought over a city. This city was a very large metropolitan city with skyscrapers and people bustling about. I observed that there was a plethora of activity transpiring in this megalopolis. There was much activity and business, but this city was dark. It wasn't dark because it was night; it was dark because there were ominous dark grey and black clouds that were present. I had the impression in my spirit that these clouds were weighty and represented bondage and oppression. In addition, these dark and foreboding clouds blocked out the sun from shining its light onto the city. I had a strong sensing of spiritual heaviness, bondage, and oppression that was associated with what I witnessed in these clouds.

I remember feeling very uneasy and even a sense of fear and terror as I looked out over this shadowy bustling landscape. People walked the streets dressed in black garments and they appeared emotionless and without joy. I began to feel the purposelessness that they possessed within the fiber of their beings. These citizens were busy, yet lacked joy and any sense of destiny. The entire scene that played out was very cold, dark, and dire. This city and its future appeared very grim.

Suddenly, my attention shifted as I heard the cracking of thunder. As my perspective shifted, I saw a Man on a white horse riding toward the city. I'll never forget the first time I saw His face in my dream. This Man was radiant with fire in his eyes, hair white as wool, and clothed in armor. He was like a warrior aggressively wielding a two-edged sword while emitting a thunderous and forceful battle-cry. The magnificence and glory of this Man was heavenly. This man was undeniably Jesus, the King of Kings, Lord of Lords, and the Captain of the Armies of Heaven in all His splendor. I was totally and completely awestruck at what I saw in this moment.

Jesus was not alone riding toward this city. No, not at all; quite the contrary. Not far behind our Savior was an army that was marching in rank and order. This army was different than any I had ever seen before. There was something incredibly peculiar about them. They were not wearing armor, fatigues, or any other sort of militaristic paraphernalia. This army wore plain, normal, regular everyday clothes. I saw people in hospital scrubs, suits and ties, sports uniforms, dresses, and uniforms from different large national corporations. This army, led by Jesus, marched in unity toward the city. They marched with force, purpose, and intensity. Jesus and His army were on a mission. Nothing was going to stop them from seeing their goal, their destiny, and their purpose accomplished!

Once this force reached the city, Jesus, the Captain of the Army, would point His sword toward a building. Upon His direction, a regiment would separate from the pack they were marching with. This regiment that was being deployed was dressed in the same manner of clothing that was associated with the structure. For example, I saw people in the attire of nurses in scrubs and doctors with stethoscopes around their neck entering a hospital. As a brigade entered a building, a blinding light began to radiate from the edifice. This light began on the ground floor and traversed up the structure until it finally erupted from the top of the roof. Light exploding forth penetrated the dark, ominous, depressing clouds that hovered overhead. Upon this light breaking through the clouds, the sun began to shine down upon the city. The light shining down dispelled the darkness. The light breaking onto the city brought about a sense of joy, hope, and peace.

One by one, building by building, battalion by battalion, I watched this entire city transformed by this legion led by Jesus.

Once every building had been invaded by this great army and transformation was released, all the clouds were rolled back. Suddenly, the entire city looked different. Now the people who were once emotionless and joyless were completely and totally transformed as they were touched by the rays emitting from the once blocked sun.

The people were now filled with joy. It was apparent these citizens now had a sense of purpose, peace, and destiny upon their lives. Even the appearance of their clothes changed. They were no longer clothed in all black as if they were en route to a funeral. Now they were dressed in multi-colored clothing that almost glowed in appearance. Everything for this metropolis had been changed in a moment. In a very short period of time, Jesus and the army that accompanied Him had made a serious shift in the people, landscape, and culture. It was a glorious sequence of events.

I awakened suddenly. I then heard the Lord speak this to my heart: **"I am raising up a transformation generation in the earth today."** At that moment, I realized this was the answer to the question He had posed to me. This was the purpose for the double portion generation. This was the entire purpose of a lifestyle of sonship. It wasn't simply to possess a powerful anointing; it was to release an anointing. It's not just about being transformed; it's about releasing transformation. It's not just about having your life revolutionized; it's about releasing a revolution. Suddenly, the picture became crystal clear to me.

Time passed—nearly two years to be exact. I shared this dream on a couple of occasions, and I even preached messages in which I detailed this dream. However, that was essentially the end of it. There was nothing else of major note, then something happened to light a fresh spark in my spirit once again.

Instant Replay

In March of 2016, while in Panama City on a trip to minister at our High Praise campus in the panhandle of Florida, I had this dream once again. It was like watching a replay of what I had dreamed before. There was the dark city, Jesus, the army marching behind him, and ultimately the transformation process of the city and its inhabitants. It was a frame by frame, scene by scene, exact replication of what I dreamed before. However, there was one major difference this time. The change wasn't in what I saw in the dream, but rather something that happened afterward.

When I awakened, I heard an addendum to what was spoken to me two years prior in Georgia. I once again heard the Lord say, "I am raising up a transformation generation in the earth today." However, God continued to speak on and added this to His previous declaration, "A generation of REVOLUTIONARIES is arising to declare freedom to the captives."

Something within my spirit leapt. I felt as if lightning shot through my spirit when I heard Father God say this. This is what it is all about: **a remarkable, tangible, and noted change released in society and culture through a generation of Holy Spirit raised up revolutionaries.** The Lord continued to say this to me repeatedly for the next several weeks. It was a declaration made to me that I couldn't shake.

Everywhere I looked I saw revolution. Even in popular culture, the ideas of revolution seemed to be everywhere I looked. It seemed there was an evolving of revolutionary men and women coming on the scene. Every thought I had ended in thinking about godly revolutionaries arising in the earth. It became an inescapable theme.

I believe that God means business and that He is raising up these revolutionaries in this hour. We have reached a point where there must be a spiritual revolution in our culture. There is no other alternative. The coming revolution is going to be led by a generation that God is releasing into their destiny and purpose to be reformers.

The Purpose of Prophetic Dreams

While there may be some who read this dream and think that it is just some insignificant sequence of images that are experienced during rapid eye movement sleep, I believe my experience was much more than random images. I know beyond a shadow of a doubt that this dream was more than just a "pizza dream." I believe it was divinely orchestrated to reveal God's heart and plans. Certainly, not every dream that we experience has spiritual consequence. However, that doesn't mean that we do not have dreams of great spiritual significance. God speaks to us in dreams. We see this fact both declared and illustrated in Scripture. As a matter of fact, dreams and visions were mentioned during the very first sermon at the birthing of the early Church. Let's take a look:

> But Peter, standing up with the eleven, raised his voice and said to them, "Men of Judea and all who dwell in Jerusalem, let this be known to you, and heed my words. For these are not drunk, as you suppose, since it is only the third hour of the day. But this is what was spoken by the prophet Joel:

> And it shall come to pass in the last days, says God, That I will pour out of My Spirit on all flesh; Your sons and your daughters shall prophesy, Your young men shall see visions, Your old men shall dream dreams. And on My menservants and on My maidservants I will pour out My Spirit in those days; And they shall prophesy (Acts 2:14-18).

How interesting that Peter mentions dreams, visions, and prophecy during his first sermon after being filled with the Holy Spirit. It is one of the very first things that he references in this discourse. I believe this is fascinating? I certainly find it to be of significance.

Peter, the man whom Jesus said possessed the rock upon which He would build the Church (Matthew 16:18), quoted a prophecy given by the prophet Joel (Joel 2:28-29). Could it be that there is a correlation between dreams and visions and the prophetic voice of God within our lives? Absolutely! I believe this truth is abundantly clear from this passage of Scripture. It takes not much more than a cursory reading to realize this fact.

Peter was announcing that the day of which Joel prophesied had arrived. This day in Jerusalem birthed a new dispensation—a new system of order. We are still living in that dispensation of grace today. God still speaks to us in dreams and visions in the same manner that Peter declared. One way that God reveals his prophetic purposes is through dreams.

It is important to realize and understand what comprises the prophetic ministry. While there are many incredible books with great detail about prophetic ministry (***Prophets and Personal Prophecy*** by Dr. Bill Hamon is a personal favorite of mine), I believe it is necessary to explain the nature of the prophetic ministry in pure form. A succinct definition of the prophetic ministry follows: it is God's plan and will being revealed to us through the working of the Holy Spirit within our lives.

When I experienced this prophetic dream in Atlanta and then in Panama City, it was more than God just giving me a good show while I slept. This dream was more than God's idea of entertainment. Moreover, it was not God showing me something just to make me feel good. Nor was it God dangling a proverbial carrot in front of me while knowing I could have no hope of experiencing this transformation. The Heavenly Father was revealing insight into His plan and will. God was displaying what He wants to do in the earth in this day, season, and hour. God desires to lead a generation of revolutionaries who will transform entire cities and usher in His transforming glory!

Revolutionaries Arising

I want to declare to you that in this day and hour, God is raising up a generation that is completely sold out to Him. He is raising up a generation who are a people of His presence. He is raising up a generation full of His power. He is raising up a generation dedicated for His purposes. He is raising up a generation who has no room for fear. He is raising up a generation of warriors. God is raising up a generation of revolutionaries.

There is a generation arising that will turn the world upside down. These revolutionaries have been faithful in the little; they have been faithful in the process of sonship. Because of their faithfulness, God is preparing to exalt them. As they arise in the earth, they will wreak havoc on the kingdoms of darkness and bring transformation to the present culture.

I believe that you are called to be part of that generation. I do not believe it is by coincidence that you are reading this book. Whether you bought it for yourself, someone gave it to you as a gift, you found it lying in a pile of other books at a thrift store, or it was picked up out of curiosity, you are reading this for a purpose. I want you to join me on this journey and let God begin to mold you, make you, and fashion you into a revolutionary.

What is a revolutionary? What does it look like to turn the world upside down? Why is this needed? These are all questions that we will address in this book as you embark on this journey of the revolutionary. I pray that you allow our Heavenly Father to speak to you and that you begin to realize you are called for more than what is normal in our culture. You are called to be a REVOLUTIONARY!

CHAPTER 2

TURN IT UPSIDE DOWN

I am a proud American citizen. As an American citizen, when I hear the word revolutionary, the first things that immediately spring into my mind are pictures of George Washington, Thomas Jefferson, Thomas Paine, Patrick Henry, Alexander Hamilton, and other well-known patriots from the late 1700's. These men were willing to lay down their lives for the cause of liberty and freedom.

If you are a citizen of the United States of America, you owe the great patriots and revolutionaries of the American War for Independence a great debt of gratitude and honor. Why? It is because this great nation would not exist as a free nation without these brilliant, brave, and prodigious men. These men hold such a great deal of esteem in my mind and heart because of the process they endured, and the obstacles they overcame on their road to establishing and ratifying the vision they had of a free and independent nation. Without these honorable men, we would not be in the position we are in as a country today. The freedoms that we are so blessed to have and engage in would be virtually non-existent.

I have often thought about these patriots and the conviction of truth that they possessed within themselves to endure adversity and see the United States established. Understand that in order to possess what we have in America today, these men had to face-off and go to war with the greatest fighting force on the earth at the time: the British Army.

These colonies could not simply walk away from the motherland, England, and expect anything other than a fight. To declare independence from the Crown was an act of sedition, rebellion, and treason. To break free from the oppression of King George III equated to signing their own death warrants. It was going to mean war. In this coming confrontation, it either meant total victory or the experience of a short drop and a quick stop at the end of a rope.

These thirteen colonies were filled with farmers. They were certainly no match for the army and navy of the kingdom of Great Britain. The colonies knew one simple fact before declaring their independence: they were completely and totally outmanned, outgunned, outnumbered, and out-planned. What would they do? Was independence and freedom worth the potential cost? This was a question that demanded introspection, debate, and ultimately an answer. Today, I am so glad they answered the way that they did. Freedom and liberty were worth any potential cost that would have to be paid.

Independence was proposed to the Continental Congress on July 2, 1776, in Philadelphia, Pennsylvania, through an early draft of the Declaration of Independence. Twelve of the thirteen colonies were in favor of Independence immediately. However, debate over independence raged on for the next two days. General George Washington, the Commander in Chief of the Continental Army, and the man who would eventually become the first President of the United States, wrote this in his General Orders on the same day that a vote was held to ratify the Declaration of Independence:

> The time is now near at hand which must probably determine, whether Americans are to be, Freemen, or Slaves; whether they are to have any property they can call their own; whether their Houses, and Farms, are to be pillaged and destroyed, and they consigned to a State of Wretchedness from which no human efforts will probably deliver them. The fate of unborn Millions will now depend, under God, on the Courage and Conduct of this army—Our cruel and unrelenting Enemy leaves us no choice but a brave resistance, or the most abject submission; this is all we can expect—We have therefore to resolve to conquer or die: Our own Country's Honor, all call upon us for a vigorous and manly exertion, and if we now shamefully fail, we shall become infamous to the whole world. Let us therefore rely upon the goodness of the Cause, and the aid of the supreme Being, in whose hands Victory is, to animate and encourage us to great and noble Actions—The Eyes of all our Countrymen are now upon us, and we shall have their blessings, and praises, if happily we are the instruments of saving them from the Tyranny meditated against them. Let us therefore animate and encourage each other, and shew the whole world, that a Freeman contending for LIBERTY on his own ground is superior to any slavish mercenary on earth.

A choice was laid down by General Washington. Freedom or slavery, independence or control? Thankfully, our founders made the correct choice: the choice for freedom and independence. On July 4, 1776, Thomas Jefferson presented a completed version of the Declaration of Independence. Fifty-six men signed the Declaration of Independence between July 4, 1776, and January 22, 1777, including two future presidents (John Adams and Thomas Jefferson) and three future vice presidents (John Adams, Elbridge Gerry, and Thomas Jefferson). Other signers of this historic document included Samuel Adams, Benjamin Rush, Benjamin Franklin, Robert Paine, among many other great patriots.

These exquisite and brilliant men were now no longer mere citizens under the rule of the crown of King George III. These incredible men now wore a title of "revolutionary." They wore it with great honor and prestige. They were no longer merely farmers, philosophers, and politicians; they were now warriors. This eclectic gathering of men were now revolutionaries. Very quickly, the spirit of revolution spread within the now thirteen United States of America. Men signed up to fight for the freedom that had been declared, and fight they did for many years.

The Siege of Yorktown

Fighting between the United States of America and the mighty kingdom of Great Britain would commence and continue for years until finally there was a culmination of this conflict. Everything would come to an effectual end at Yorktown, Virginia. The world was about to be turned upside down by these colonial Americans.

With General Cornwallis of the kingdom of Great Britain taking up quarters in Yorktown, the time was right for General Washington to strike and potentially end the revolution. If successful, this strike could see freedom from the rule of The Crown realized once and for all. The revolutionaries had been able to illicit help from the French, gaining soldiers, guns, and probably most importantly, ships from the Navy of France. This was the game-changer that they needed. Lieutenant General Rochambeau from France joined forces with General George Washington to strategize the siege of Yorktown. This attack would be an assault that could effectively ensure independence and end the American Revolution if they gained victory. They had but one shot at triumph and they were not going to throw it away.

On October 17, 1781, Washington and Rochambeau began their siege of Yorktown. After days of fighting, a young British drummer marched toward the American army. This drummer was followed closely by a British officer waving the white flag of surrender. Realizing that defeat was inevitable, Cornwallis sent word to Washington desiring to discuss terms of capitulation. On October 19, 1781, the articles of capitulation were signed. Signatories of the document included Washington, Rochambeau, the Comte de Barras (on behalf of the French Navy), Cornwallis, and Thomas Symonds (the senior Royal Navy officer present).

On their surrender, the red coats marched from Yorktown to the rhythm and sound of the drum and fife playing. While the army from across the Atlantic Ocean marched away in defeat they sang a song. The name of the song was "The World Turned Upside Down." How appropriate and prophetic this was. This course of events and these revolutionaries had caused the entire world to be turned on its head. The world had been truly and effectively turned upside down. There was a new nation, a new power, and a new normal throughout the world.

When Lord North, British Prime Minister was notified of the surrender of General Cornwallis to Washington and Rochambeau, he is reported to have exclaimed, "Oh God, it's all over." The American War for Independence had been effectively and soundly won. The revolution was over and victory had been attained. The treaty of Paris would later be signed on September 3, 1783. This formally ended the conflict.

More Than History

I want you to realize that I have not spent the last several pages talking about the revolution to simply give you a recounting of history. You most likely learned these things in primary school. While I consider myself a bit of a history nerd and believe we should all probably be more versed in those who have come before us, there is a purpose for you reading these accounts of the American Revolution. I believe there is great spiritual significance we can find in the account of the Siege of Yorktown.

There were prophetic pictures and statements made by the defeated Redcoats as they identified the attributes of true revolutionaries. There is one key statement that I want to focus on that is credited to both the revolutionaries in colonial America and to the church in the Book of Acts. They have a major characteristic in common. The enemies of both the early Church and the colonial revolutionaries prophetically identified them. What was their identifying attribute? They were proclaimed to be those who **turn the world upside down**. Let's look at how that very attribute was imputed upon Paul, Silas, and the entire early church in Thessalonica.

> Now when they had passed through Amphipolis and Apollonia, they came to Thessalonica, where there

> was a synagogue of the Jews. Then Paul, as his custom was, went in to them, and for three Sabbaths reasoned with them from the Scriptures, explaining and demonstrating that the Christ had to suffer and rise again from the dead, and saying, "This Jesus whom I preach to you is the Christ." And some of them were persuaded; and a great multitude of the devout Greeks, and not a few of the leading women, joined Paul and Silas. But the Jews who were not persuaded, becoming envious, took some of the evil men from the marketplace, and gathering a mob, set all the city in an uproar and attacked the house of Jason, and sought to bring them out to the people. But when they did not find them, they dragged Jason and some brethren to the rulers of the city, crying out, **"these who have turned the world upside down have come here too"** (Acts 17:1-6, emphasis added).

The Common Thread

I hope you see the common thread that links the patriots of the American Revolution and the early Church in the Book of Acts. What is it? They both turned the world upside down! While the Redcoats put this identification on the American troops, it is disgruntled people from the systems of the world that put this badge of honor upon Paul and Silas.

You must understand that Thessalonica, the location where Paul and Silas have this said of them, is a port city. In port cities, there were people that traversed from all over the surrounding regions and areas. I believe that Paul and Silas, as well as the entirety of the early church, lived in such a state of revival and establishing the kingdom of God that they were causing a dismantling of the systems of the world.

In Thessalonica, they had heard about Paul pronouncing blindness on the sorcerer Bar-Jesus (Elymas) in Paphos and thus leading the Proconsul of Rome to salvation (Acts 13:6-12). The people there had heard about the teaching of Paul at Antioch who preached with great conviction and truth in that city. Paul enraged religious leaders, but the end result was both Jew and Gentile being born again (Acts 13:13-48). Miracles were being manifested through Paul. In Lystra, he proclaimed to a crippled man, "Stand up straight on your feet!" The crippled man began to leap and walked uprightly (Acts 14:8-9). Surely Thessalonica had heard about this astonishing sign.

I would be willing to wager that they had heard about another event in Lystra as well. After seeing miracles, Paul was stoned to death. That's right, they killed him. However, you can't keep a good man down. The next day Paul rose from the dead and went back to ministering once again (Acts 14:19-20). That is incredible determination and commitment to the call of God.

Lastly, I'm sure they had heard of a recent development where Paul cast the spirit of divination out of a young slave. This working of deliverance certainly cost her masters greatly. Paul had taken away their money maker and meal-ticket. As a result, Paul and Silas were beaten and thrown in prison. Not being ones to ever be defeated, they worshipped the Lord in prison and their chains were broken. Moreover, they were not content to just leave the jail. Instead, they preached the word of the Lord to the Philippian jailer and his entire household was saved and baptized (Acts 16:16-34).

Paul was messing up everything for the societal and religious ruling class. This apostle—this prophet—this revolutionary—was turning everything upside down everywhere he placed his foot. Surely, as a port city, the rulers, magistrates, and religious class had heard what Paul was doing. Hearing these accounts, the last thing they wanted was the presence of the former Saul of Tarsus in their city. When Paul does show up in Thessalonica he begins to preach. This results in change throughout the city. Gentiles (Greeks), who pride themselves in their intellect, begin to be converted. Women begin to follow the teaching of Paul and Silas. They are wrecking everything within the worldly systems in Thessalonica.

In the same manner that Paul, Silas, and the Church in their day were identified as ones who were turning the world upside down, Washington and the American revolutionaries would be identified in the same manner. Why? It is because this is the identity and mission of true men and women filled with the spirit of revolution. There is something about them that upsets the status-quo and causes a change in every arena of society they encounter.

What is a Revolutionary?

I don't want to simply speak in abstracts, so I would like to give identification to what I mean when I say revolutionary. Merriam-Webster dictionary was founded and first written by Noah Webster. He served in the Connecticut militia during the Revolutionary War. Webster defines a revolutionary this way:

Revolutionary - of, relating to, or constituting a revolution, tending to or promoting revolution, constituting or bringing about a major or fundamental change.

The root word of "revolutionary" is the word "revolution." Moreover, revolution is defined in Merriam-Webster dictionary in this manner:

Revolution - as a sudden, radical, or complete change.

I want you to understand this fact: revolutionaries evoke a sudden and complete change. They bring about a radical shift in the status-quo. This is the barometer for spiritual revolutionaries: do they evoke a positive change? Revolutionaries are those who live their lives in such a way that their very presence produces a sudden and marked change everywhere they go.

Understand, if there is no change produced from our lifestyle and presence, then we have yet to enter the fullness of being a part of the spiritual revolutionary generation that God is releasing today. If we pray and things don't shift, then we haven't embraced the fullness of the mantle of the revolutionary. If we praise and the kingdoms of hell don't quake and shake, then we haven't entered the fullness of the mantle of the revolutionary. If when we come to church, we are checking our watch wondering when things are going to be finished so we can get to the buffet, then we haven't entered the fullness of the mantle of the spiritual revolutionary. I believe there is an invitation for all of us to join the ranks of the revolutionaries today.

We are called to bring forth change. We are not to merely be another person living our life for a season on this earth and then one day dying and going to heaven. While it is good to live what can be heralded as a "good life" and certainly phenomenal and important to have our place in heaven secure, the Lord has so much more for us to do and accomplish. We are called to be a history maker and a world shaker. God has not called us for normal or average. We are called to do more than just fill a seat in a local church, go home in the same condition, and evoke no change in our lives or the lives of those that we encounter daily. God has called us, anointed us, purposed us, and planned us. He is now calling us forth as a revolutionary who will turn the world upside down in this day and hour. He is calling us today, so we must answer the call to join the ranks of revolutionaries in the earth.

Jesus: The Ultimate Revolutionary

If we really stop and just think about Jesus, He was the model of a revolutionary in every sense. Our Savior was the ultimate revolutionary. Jesus brought about the greatest change in history through His redemptive, teaching, and demonstrative ministry. His ministry had multiple dimensions and brought about multiple dimensions of revolution as a result.

Jesus demonstrated a revolutionary mindset in everything He did. He was willing to undergo thirty years of preparation that very few witnessed. During this thirty years, there was no platform, no disciples, and no adoring crowds. Much like a seed under soil, there was preparation going on for blossoming, budding, and bearing fruit. This thirty years of preparation was ultimately for three years of earthly ministry. This was a revolutionary mindset. Not only did this disposition defy most logic, it was also unprecedented.

Before Jesus came to this earth, no one had ever worked miracles on the Sabbath. However, Jesus performed miracles on the Sabbath. This made those with a religious spirit very upset. Religious leaders in that age (and in our age) were self-absorbed and concerned with being served. Jesus came serving others. He washed His disciple's feet. Jesus was a picture of true servanthood. His way to triumph was not by conquest, but rather through His death.

Jesus' methodology certainly must have seemed bizarre to most. However, when you are a revolutionary, you do things differently than others. Through what seemed so different and peculiar to most, Jesus brought about the greatest revolution the world had ever seen. Not only did He defy the societal norms of His day, He defied even death. Jesus was the ultimate model of a revolutionary in everything He demonstrated and proclaimed.

Paul, Silas, Peter, and other church fathers were simply being reflective of what Jesus demonstrated in the way they lived. They were living a life of mirroring what Jesus did—evoking revolution. No longer were they living in the manner of everyone else. The revolutionaries of the early church were living lives that were provoking change.

Reject Normal

Revolutionaries are not normal. Understand this simple fact; we were not created for a normal or average existence. We were not created to be like everyone else in all of society. We were made to be different. Jesus told Peter that He would "build His church" (Matthew 16:18). The word translated as "church" is the Greek word *ekklesia* which means *a calling out*.

We were called out of sin. We were called out of transgression. However, let me add one more proclamation from which we have been called out: we were called out of normal. We were never called to fit in. We were intended and created to be different. What is normal for everyone in society and in the world, is not the envisioned result for us.

Sin is normal to the flesh, but the moment we were born-again you ceased being normal. Therefore, sin should not be part of our everyday life. We were given a new nature. We were given a new mantle. We were called out to be a revolutionary. Complacency is normal to the flesh. However, we aren't of the flesh, we are of the Spirit. Conformity is normal to the flesh, but we were not created for conformity. Remember, as a revolutionary, we are purposed to turn the world upside down.

In the New Testament, this proclamation is made over us as believers, "But ye are a chosen generation, a royal priesthood, a holy nation, a *peculiar people*; that ye should shew forth the praises of him who hath called you out of darkness into his marvelous light" (1 Peter 2:9, KJV, emphasis added). The Greek word translated as "peculiar" is *eis*. It means *far more exceeding for intent and purpose*. God has a far more exceedingly glorious intent and purpose for us than what the world defines as normal. I would also say this: God has a greater plan for us than what the average American church culture has defined as acceptable and normal. We were created for more. If our spirit man yearns for more than what we may currently be experiencing with God, we are already burning with the mantle of a revolutionary.

In our modern church culture, many view the gathering of believers as more of a country club than an equipping center. We aren't designed for just some sort of social club. That is not what I see as being the model for the Church. The ultimate model to be followed is the Church in the Book of Acts. I don't see Peter, Paul, Barnabas, Silas, and Apollos having donuts and video games to gather a crowd. What I see is a people who are turning the world upside down. I see people moving in miracles, signs, and wonders. I see a people who are affecting societal change. I see a people who are different and peculiar.

It is okay to be different than the culture. As a matter of fact, if we are nothing more than a mirror of the culture, we are presently disqualified from being a revolutionary. Only when we change can we begin to fight on the front lines of revolution. Those who are called to be on the front lines of revolution are different than most. Revolutionaries will act different and talk different. Thus, they have a different outcome to their lives. I want to implore you with this: **REJECT NORMAL**.

When I see what Jesus said about believers, it is far removed from what others seem to call "normal." Jesus said this:

> And these signs will follow those who believe: In My name they will cast out demons; they will speak with new tongues; they will take up serpents; and if they drink anything deadly, it will by no means hurt them; they will lay hands on the sick, and they will recover" (Mark 16:17-18).

This is far from what most call normal. However, Jesus communicated that this was a new normal that He was establishing for all of those who believe. Notice, He did not say these signs will follow those who are in full-time ministry.

Jesus simply said that these are the signs that would follow those that believe.

If we are followers of Jesus, we should be seeing the miraculous manifest. Do we believe the words of Jesus or the doctrine of contemporary culture? Do we want to see what Jesus promised, or are we content with what everyone else says is "normal"? As for me and my house, we are rejecting normal, and we are making the choice to embrace the mantle of the revolutionary in this day.

Change That Endures

When I begin to think about the world being turned upside down by Washington, Adams, and the other revolutionaries, I had this realization. Today, we are still benefitting from the fruit of their revolution. I am an independent and free American citizen largely because of the stand they took. When you observe the early church, we are still benefitting from them turning the world upside down. The writings and examples they established have shaped our idea and philosophy concerning what it means to be a Christian. Besides Jesus, Paul's spiritual revelation in all things pertaining to Christianity is the greatest influence in all of Christendom.

Certainly, when we look at Jesus we are still living under a change that He evoked in the heavenlies and the earth through a spiritual revolution. We would be lost and on our way to hell without the intervention that Jesus brought forth. Hallelujah! I am so thankful for the spirit of revolution that these men activated and walked in through their lives.

I believe in the same manner exhibited by these incredible men, God is raising up a generation that will lead a revolution that can endure. I believe the day of the "flash in the pan" revival is over. No more will we see people gather to have meetings for a short time and then witness everything return to the same decrepit and broken state that it was previously. For so long, there have been those who claim to have the spirit of revival and revolution, yet there is no fruit to accompany their declaration. At best, the accompanying fruit is incredibly short-lived—withering away just as quickly as it sprung forth. I prophesy that this generation will not repeat this same pattern.

This generation of revolutionaries will have true fruit. True revolution will produce more than a passing emotional experience. The fruit that is produced from revolution will therefore be fruit that remains. Jesus said, "You should go and bear fruit, and that your fruit should remain" (John 15:16). This is still His desire today, for the fruit of revolution to remain and endure the test of time and generations.

I believe that future history books will point to this generation as a turn-around generation: a generation of revolutionaries. These revolutionaries are going to see transformation take place that future generations will reflect upon and remember with the fondness, honor, and respect that we equate with the church in the Book of Acts. These revolutionaries will not fail or falter, but they will accomplish their purpose within the earth. These revolutionaries are going to see nations changed in a moment.

> Who has heard such a thing?
> Who has seen such things?
> Shall the earth be made to give birth in one day?

> Or shall a nation be born at once?
> For as soon as Zion was in labor,
> She gave birth to her children (Isaiah 66:8).

Revolutionaries are being birthed in the earth today. They possess a divine purpose, identity, and destiny. Let the revolutionaries arise in the Church and be released into the world!

CHAPTER 3

REVIVAL: THE LYNCHPIN OF REVOLUTION

Will You not revive us again,
That Your people may rejoice in You?
Show us Your mercy, Lord,
And grant us Your salvation (Psalm 85:6-7).

This Psalm was written shortly after the miraculous event in which Israel had returned from Babylonian captivity in the days of Zerubbabel. While we do not have the exact name of the author, it is apparent he is a patriot of Israel who is beseeching the Lord for restoration of Israel to a former glory, a glory of which this generation had only heard. Though they were no longer in bondage to the enemy, they still needed a refreshing. They needed revival.

I believe the state of the Hebrews in this chapter is an incredible parallel picture of the current condition of the body of Christ at large. We are no longer in bondage to the enemy, but in dire need of a reviving. I have read the book of Acts and the state of His Church during that day. I've read the history of great men of reformation like Martin Luther, John Wesley, Charles Wesley, Charles Finney, George Whitefield, William Seymour, and so many others throughout the history of the Church. Though there are portions of the body of Christ that are experiencing incredible levels of renewing, it is the will of God for the entirety of His body to be revived. We need revival! We must have an awakening!

I have good news for you today. God wants to revive His people. While it presently appears to be a great time of slumber among the people of God, the answer to spiritual lethargy is the alarm clock of revival. Understand this: as much as we may desire to see the Church awakened in the earth today, God desires it even more. Why? It is because without the Church waking up she can never become the agent of authority and restoration that the Father has called her to be within society and culture. For this reason, I believe that we are on the precipice of the greatest revival and outpouring that this world has ever seen.

Without the influence of Christians operating in kingdom authority, society will continue to deteriorate and ultimately end up in total collapse. Just look through history at any and every culture that has turned its back on God. You will not have to look through very much antiquity to find great societies that abandoned God. These great empires have suffered the same fate: collapse.

All cultures that have denied God and His working have ultimately crumbled quickly. Let this not be said of my nation; let this not be said of your nation. We must take our rightful place in influencing and setting the tone for culture. There is only one way for this to be birthed: revival in the Church that effects the society. Without the influence of the Church, the kingdom of God can never be established on the earth in the manner which the Lord desires.

Throughout history we have seen some incredible outpourings: the Welsh revival, the Toronto blessing, the Brownsville revival, and both Great Awakenings just to name a few. As incredible and glorious as those revivals have been, those are only a small taste of what will happen in the days to come. I believe that the latter will be greater than the former.

In my spirit, I see a worldwide revival with believers being awakened to purpose, destiny, and relationship with the Lord. God is releasing a revival unlike anything the world has ever seen! We will see a time of refreshing that was prophesied and declared by Peter in Acts 3:19. Times of refreshing and renewal are being released from the presence of the Lord. Why is this going to transpire? It is because God desires to bring a reformation and revolution unlike anything we have ever seen in days past. The revival must come before revolution and reformation. Why? It is because revival is the seedbed of revolution.

Bursting My Bubble

I want to tell you of an experience that took place in my life. I can remember it like it was yesterday. I was sitting in a church listening to a minister preach. This gentleman spoke with authority, humor, and knowledge. He had a whiteboard and was feverishly writing, creating flow charts and diagrams. This preacher was lecturing about the need for reformation in our culture today. He eloquently described how we needed to see a kingdom of God invasion in every arena of society. This minister of the gospel was totally speaking my language; my interest was piqued.

This gentleman continued to say that we needed a revolution in our culture. I couldn't have agreed more with what he was saying. I was on the edge of my seat with excitement. With every word that proceeded from his mouth, I was more and more in total agreement with what he expounded in this powerful sermon. He continued and said something that I will never forget. He said, "Revival is not the answer; we've had revivals, and they didn't produce lasting change." Suddenly, I felt as if I had been kicked in the gut. The chair had seemingly been pulled from underneath me.

What had begun as excitement to hear someone echoing the sentiment that I felt so strongly in my heart with regard to revolution and reformation, soon turned to disappointment and disillusionment. I was excited as I listened to him. Then something happened during his discourse; it took an unexpected turn. This man began to deride the very idea of revival. At one point, he even began to openly mock those who were praying, contending, and warring to see revival. I was stunned. I was shocked. I was perplexed.

For many years I had heard respected ministers of the gospel preach and proclaim that we must have revival in our society. I had spent countless hours praying for our nation and the nations of the earth to experience the greatest revival the world had ever known. At the time, I was a youth pastor and had routinely told the students I was pastoring that the solution for the hurdles our culture was facing could only be found inside a Christ-centered revival. Was I wrong? Had I missed it? Revival certainly couldn't be a bad thing? Certainly, God wants to revive his people, the nations of the world, and the inhabitants therein, doesn't He?

I wasn't entirely sure what to do with what I had just heard. Is revival necessary, or do we just need revolution? Over the course of the next several months, I took an introspective journey. I arrived at this conclusion: revival is a necessity for us today. As much as I believe in reformation and revolution, we will never get there unless we go through the soil of revival. It's not choosing revolution or revival; it's choosing both. We need revolution and revival. We don't have to choose one or the other. There is no need to pit revival and revolution against one another; they go hand in hand.

Defining Revival

Before we go any further in this chapter and line of reflection, it is important to define what revival is and is not. Without proper understanding, we cannot comprehend and enunciate the reasoning for the importance of true revival.

First of all, understand what revival is not. You may have attended a series of meetings over the course of a week at a local church that were called "revival services." There may have been elements of revival that took place at these meetings. However, revival is more than just a continual series of meetings that takes place. Simply having church services for a week straight does not necessarily constitute a true revival.

Revival is not people crying at an altar. Revival is not people dancing during praise and worship. Revival is not people praying with fervency. Revival is not congregants suddenly starting to attend a church. These things are the byproduct of revival, but they are not revival defined at its very core.

Revival simply defined is a re-awakening. Understand this fact, revival comes for the believer not the unbeliever. Many reason in their minds that revival is manifested for the unbeliever. However, this is not the case. The word "revive," which is the root word for "revival," means *restore to life or consciousness, give new strength or energy to*. If someone is unconscious and then brought back to a state of cognizance, we would say that they were revived. The reason we say they were revived is because they returned to the condition in which they were previously living. Let me describe it like this: for something to be revived, life must have been present at some point.

Revival comes for the believer that has already been resurrected spiritually from the place of death, but is currently not at a state of being fully awake and productive. The Church must come back to life, return to her first love, and do the first works. This is what Jesus told the church of Ephesus in Revelation, a congregation that needed revival.

> "To the angel of the church of Ephesus write, 'These things says He who holds the seven stars in His right hand, who walks in the midst of the seven golden lampstands: "I know your works, your labor, your patience, and that you cannot bear those who are evil. And you have tested those who say they are apostles and are not, and have found them liars; and you have persevered and have patience, and have labored for My name's sake and have not become weary. Nevertheless I have this against you, that you have left your first love. Remember therefore from where you have fallen; repent and do the first works, or else I will come to you quickly and remove your lampstand from its place—unless you repent"'" (Revelation 2:1-5).

This is such a picture of the church in the world today. We have good programs. We have been patient. We have endured, and we certainly work hard. Nevertheless, something is missing. We must return to our first love just as Jesus prompted the church in Ephesus. We must do the first works.

What were the first works of the church? We should look at the church in the Book of Acts. After all, they are the first people to work as God's church on the earth. I believe we see the first works through the lives of Peter, Paul, Silas, and other early church leaders. How were they functioning and operating? They were operating in healing, signs, wonders, miracles, deliverance, and an expression of the supernatural power of God! **The first works of the early church caused the world to be TURNED UPSIDE DOWN!** (Acts 17:6)

Revival is a radical encounter with our first love, Jesus. That encounter naturally leads to the first works—the expression of His supernatural power within the earth. It's time we have revival and have the intended and desired effect of heaven on earth. God still desires that His Church turn the world upside down in this very day and hour!

When followers of Jesus experience true revival, it causes them to rise from a state of inactivity and begin to operate in the fullness of the Christian life. Instead of leaning to the arm of the flesh, they begin to allow the Holy Spirit to guide them in all aspects of life. This shifting of priorities causes people to begin to manifest Jesus everywhere they go. Thus, everyone they encounter is affected by the awakening that has transpired in the heart of the believer.

The revival that has happened within their hearts and lives begins to bring revolution everywhere they go. Jesus and the presence of His Spirit manifested in our lives brings forth a reviving that then enables and empowers us to be agents of revolution in the earth.

No Revolution Without Revival

Revival and revolution are intricately connected and linked. Without revival coming first, any revolution will be short-lived and ineffective. Moreover, if revival is nothing more than a series of meetings, it has fallen short of reaching the fullness of its inherent potential. If a revival does not birth revolutionaries, the purpose has been missed altogether. **Revival comes to wake up the proper personnel that are needed for revolution.**

I believe that the seed of transformation—the seed of revolution—is on the inside of every believer. The principle of the seed is important in Christianity. Let's look at what Jesus said about the seed.

> Another parable He put forth to them, saying: "The kingdom of heaven is like a mustard seed, which a man took and sowed in his field, which indeed is the least of all the seeds; but when it is grown it is greater than the herbs and becomes a tree, so that the birds of the air come and nest in its branches" (Matthew 13:31-32).

Here, Jesus is revealing to us the importance and power of the seed. Everything eternal, everything of worth in life, operates by the principle of the seed. The kingdom of heaven is likened unto the seed. Therefore, everything in the kingdom operates by this same principle. Our life is like a seed. The lifestyle of a spiritual revolutionary is like a seed. The revolutionary seed within our lives must be properly planted and watered in order to yield the fruit of revolution.

One of most important things for seed is the soil in which it is planted. If seed is not deposited in proper soil, the potential of fruit will remain locked inside of the seed. Revolutionary seed must be deposited in the ground of the culture of revival to produce fruit.

The moment we are born-again, all the potential to produce revolution in our arena of influence is imparted to us. However, it is in seed form locked inside of our spirit. Unfortunately, many never produce the sudden, effective, or lasting change for which they are called and destined. Why? It is because the seed of revolution was never planted in the soil of revival. Only seed that is planted properly buds, blossoms, and produces fruit.

We do not have to make the choice between revival and revolution; they are two sides of the same coin. Without revival, there is no revolution, and all revival should proceed and end in revolution. Revolution in society and its systems is the fruit of the lifestyle of the believer planted in revival. There is no other path to effective and lasting positive change in our society.

This is what we see in the American Revolution. We observe a group of men and women who experienced revival. We could say that they were planted in the soil of revival. This birthed revolution. Let me show you.

From Great Awakening to Revolution

As of late, I have been drawing so much inspiration and encouragement from the lives of the historical figures that were of great importance to the American Revolution. This has led me to do a lot of study into causes and provocation that led to the War for Independence. I have found many interesting things that I was not taught in former history classes when I learned about men like Benjamin Franklin, George Washington, Thomas Jefferson, and other revolutionaries of the late 1700's. Let me share with you what I have discovered during my research.

I was always taught that the revolution was primarily provoked by taxation without representation in Parliament. Essentially, Great Britain wanted to get as much money as possible out of the original thirteen colonies without giving much in return. The colonies protested what they felt was unjust, and this led them down the road of revolution.

These things are all true and did factually happen. However, there were motivating factors deeper and more intrinsic. There were spiritual motivators in which the revolution was rooted that were greater than any political motivator. To look closer at these factors, we must go back even further in time than 1776. We must return all the way back to the first major revival to visit the shores of America: the Great Awakening.

In the 1730's and 1740's a revival swept across Protestant Europe, but especially the American colonies. This was a true revival in the sense that those primarily reached were people who were already members of a local church. The powerful preaching from men like Jonathan Edwards, Samuel Davies, and George Whitefield, accompanied by the moving of Holy Spirit, caused all those who encountered this move of God to realize their need to have a personal relationship with Jesus. It was an authentic revival as people encountered Jesus and His presence in a tangible way. These American colonists' relationship with Jesus was no longer merely ceremonial or cultural, but their devotion to God became very real and personal.

This new-found relationship then caused them to be awakened to the authority of God within the earth. Once awakened, they began to question governmental authorities, especially the King of England and the accompanying Parliament. The seeds for what would become the revolution were planted in the soil of the First Great Awakening in colonial America. The real revolution began during the First Great Awakening. This sentiment was recorded and echoed by many great men of that day.

On February 13, 1818, President John Adams wrote a letter to Hezekiah Niles, American editor and publisher of the Baltimore-based national weekly news magazine, ***Niles' Weekly Register***. In this letter, Adams explained the influence of religion and revival on the American War for Independence. Adams penned the following to Niles:

> The Revolution was effected before the war commenced. The Revolution was in the minds and hearts of the people; a change in their religious sentiments of their duties and obligations. While the king, and all in authority under him, were believed to govern in justice and mercy, according to the laws and constitution derived to them from the

> God of nature and transmitted to them by their ancestors, they thought themselves bound to pray for the king and queen and all the royal family, and all in authority under them, as ministers ordained of God for their good; but when they saw those powers renouncing all the principles of authority, and bent upon the destruction of all the securities of their lives, liberties, and properties, they thought it their duty to pray for the continental congress and all the thirteen State congresses.
>
> ...This radical change in the principles, opinions, sentiments, and affections of the people, was the real American Revolution.

Wow! These words are from John Adams, signer of the Declaration of Independence, first Vice-President of the United States, and second President of the United States. If there is anyone qualified to speak on the motivators and root causes of the American Revolution, it is President John Adams. I assure you that the second President of the United States of America is more qualified to speak on this era of history than any collegiate American history professor or modern historian. John Adams lived through the revolution; he is an authority on the subject.

We can clearly see from this letter that the causes for rebellion against England were not simply secular, but rather were based on religious principle and revelation. Where does Adams say the American Revolution began? "The Revolution was in the minds and hearts of the people; a change in their religious sentiments of their duties and obligations." When did this change transpire? This metamorphosis of philosophy and understanding happened during the First Great Awakening.

In the period during the First Great Awakening, revivalism began to teach the colonists to challenge the authority of the Church of England. No longer bound by formalism, fervency had replaced liturgy. This revival even encouraged boldness when facing down religious authority, especially when that authority was illegitimate in nature. Most importantly, the eventual American citizens learned that if a church was no longer being faithful to the accuracy of Scripture or to the church's parishioners, they could then establish their own. It is because of this understanding that John Wesley, Charles Wesley, and George Whitefield would establish what would eventually become known as the Methodist Church in the middle of the First Great Awakening.

These understandings spilled over into government as well as religion. The spiritual understanding of the colonists influenced everything in their lives. The Great Awakening ushered in a climate in which the American Revolution would be possible.

If you need any further evidence to show the effect of religion, and specifically the Great Awakening, upon the American Revolution, look no further than the secretary to British General Howe, Ambrose Serle. Serle wrote to the British Secretary of State in 1776 and told him that the American Revolution was a religious war. Many have further asserted that the American Revolution would have crumbled without it being sustained by Presbyterian Ministers in America.

Think about the power of the pulpit—the power of the church in America. The right-hand-man of a British General, a high ranking military officer, believed that the entire revolution would crumble if it wasn't for preachers. It had nothing to do with artillery, strategy, or use of a navy. From the perspective of Ambrose Serle, it was ministers of the gospel that made the difference. Wow!

Further evidence of the influence of the pulpit is revealed straight from the throne of England itself. King George III and many other high ranking Britons did not even frequently call the war with the rebellion colonies the American Revolution. Instead, they chose to refer to the rebellion of the colonists as the "Presbyterian War." While we will not see this in any modern mini-series produced for television or read it in many books written about this era, it does not change the fact that George III, King of England, perceived that the American war was a Presbyterian rebellion. Of course, it should not be forgotten that the Presbyterian Church experienced a major revival and reformation during the First Great Awakening that swept colonial America. The ideals that began to change in their lives shaped what would eventually become the American Revolution.

Whitefield: The Voice of Awakening

There was probably none more influential in the Great Awakening than a powerful man of God named George Whitefield. Whitefield, an English born preacher, first visited the American colonies in 1738. This began a life-long, God-given assignment to reach America with the gospel and spread the fires of revival far and wide. The Great Awakening was largely sparked by Whitefield's preaching tour of America that lasted from 1739-1740.

During this time period, Whitefield preached at both Harvard and New Haven College (which we know today as Yale).

Whitefield's preaching produced such a glory that it was reported in Cambridge, Massachusetts at Harvard that "the college is entirely changed. The students are full of God." What an amazing fact! One awakened man, sparked a revolution in an entire collegiate campus. It is believed that Whitefield preached so much across the American colonies that at least eighty percent of all colonists heard him preach at some point. One such man that heard him preach was an eventual founder of the United States of America, the brilliant and wise, Benjamin Franklin. Franklin wrote of one specific encounter when hearing Whitefield preach:

> I happened soon after to attend one of his Sermons, in the Course of which I perceived he intended to finish with a Collection, and I silently resolved he should get nothing from me. I had in my Pocket a Handful of Copper Money, three or four silver Dollars, and five Pistoles [Spanish coins] in Gold. As he proceeded I began to soften, and concluded to give the Coppers. Another Stroke of his Oratory made me asham'd of that, and determin'd me to give the Silver; and he finish'd so admirably, that I emptied my Pocket wholly into the Collector's Dish, Gold and all. At this Sermon there was also one of our Club [Junto literary club], who being of my Sentiments respecting [opinions concerning] the Building in Georgia, and suspecting a Collection might be intended, had by Precaution emptied his Pockets before he came from home; toward the Conclusion of the Discourse [sermon], however, he felt a strong Desire to give, and apply'd to a Neighbor who stood near him to borrow some Money for the Purpose.

Whitefield obviously made a profound impression on Franklin and his life. Even though it is arguable that Benjamin Franklin may be the most secular of the founding fathers, it is difficult to not think that Whitefield made a major impact on the life of the man who discovered electricity. Franklin even routinely printed Whitefield's sermons on the front page of his newspaper, ***The Pennsylvania Gazette***. I do not believe that Benjamin Franklin would have printed these sermons if they didn't impact his heart in a major manner.

Furthermore, Franklin calculated that when Whitefield preached in the open streets that as many as thirty-thousand people could hear him due to how far his voice carried. Whitefield was literally a loud and boisterous voice of awakening that prompted a revolution. When we put all of this together it is no wonder that Harvard professor, William Perry said, "The Declaration of Independence of 1776 was a result of the evangelical preaching of the evangelists of the Great Awakening."

Do it Again

The early church, birthed in revival, led to revolutionaries that turned the world upside down. Moreover, the founding fathers, birthed in revival, led to revolutionaries that turned the world upside down. Revival is truly the seedbed of revolution. We are not going to stop at simply some sort of encounter with God that stays with us but for a fleeting moment. Our encounter is meant to birth something that affects everyone with whom we come into contact. We will talk about this in greater detail in our next chapter.

Understand this, revival births revolutionaries who turn the world upside down. Moreover, God will cause it to happen again today. Hallelujah! Lord, do it again! Let the seed of revolution be planted in the soil of revival!

CHAPTER 4

ENCOUNTERING THE FIRE

"The world has yet to see what God can do with
a man fully consecrated to him."
—Dwight L. Moody

I love this quote from this nineteenth century revivalist from Massachusetts. I still remember the first time I read it and how it gripped me deeply within my heart. I felt such a conviction and compulsion to be one who fulfilled this. I want my life to be a life fully consecrated to God for His purposes.

The word "consecrated" is defined by Webster's Dictionary as *something dedicated to a sacred purpose.* Thus, a consecrated life is one dedicated for the purposes of God. A consecrated life will be surrounded by the manifestation of God's glory. It will be a revolutionary life.

Still, let's take this statement by Reverend Moody one step further. I fully believe that the world has yet to see what God can do through a **generation** fully consecrated to him. I believe there can be an entire **generation** consecrated to God. Why should we settle for one single wholly consecrated individual? Dream big! Believe for big things in God! The Lord of Hosts is raising up that consecrated **generation** in our day and hour.

Radical revolutionaries that have been born in the soil of revival are going to turn the world upside down. These revolutionaries will be those who bring freedom to those held in captivity by the enemy. This is the purpose and fruit of a generation that is fully and wholly consecrated unto God for His plans and purposes. Spiritual freedom fighters, spiritual revolutionaries are arising in the earth.

In our last chapter, we talked extensively about revival. More specifically, the idea that revival comes to birth a spirit of revolution. As we have outlined, revolution is defined as a sudden, radical, or complete change. The entire purpose of revival is for that encounter to be a point of initiation to move us toward destiny. All believers are called to become awakened revolutionaries. This is part of our destiny.

Awakened ones, people of encounter, begin to herald the news of freedom and becomes leaders of liberty. This is exactly what happened within the life of Moses. Moses was truly a life that was wholly consecrated to God and he had an incredible and revolutionary effect on the earth in his time. As a matter of fact, Moses' accomplishments echo throughout all of history to this very day.

The Early Days of Moses

I'm sure that if you were raised in church or ever owned a kid's story Bible, you are probably familiar with the story of Moses. However, I have found we frequently overlook incredible truths in simple biblical accounts because we are so familiar with them. The old saying is that familiarity breeds contempt. I believe that we often become too familiar with the Word. As a result of our familiarity, we can begin to treat the Word of

God like we would treat a fictional tale we may read. We go, "Oh that was nice, how sweet." However, we miss the revelation that is packed within every verse of God's sharp, living, and active Word (Hebrews 4:12).

We should be very familiar with biblical accounts like Moses, but should never treat it with familiarity. There is a trove of treasure locked inside of this often-repeated story. We can unlock these treasures if we treat the Word with the honor, respect, and reverence it commands.

The biblical narrative of Moses and his journey to becoming a powerful and great deliverer began in the book of Exodus with him being born to an Israelite father of the tribe of Levi, the priesthood tribe. At this time, the Hebrews were slaves under Egyptian subjugation and held in bondage. The descendants of Abraham, Isaac, and Jacob were not dwelling in the land promised to them, rather they were building the empire of their enemy.

There are a host of people in the world today that are called to the kingdom, called to destiny and promise, yet they are in bondage and building the empire of the enemy. Understand, the people of Israel would have remained in bondage making bricks from straw and clay, and remained building the enemy's empire, unless a revolutionary arose. It is the same today. Those that are spiritual slaves do not simply find their way to freedom by chance. Someone must arise with the fortitude, with the conviction, and with a voice of authority to say, "LET MY PEOPLE GO." They must lead them out of captivity and bondage. Revolutionaries do just that.

Let's return to the narrative in Exodus. In the time that Moses was born, Pharaoh sent a decree ordering all Israelite male children to be thrown in the Nile River. These defenseless babies would either drown or be eaten by crocodiles that inhabited the body of water. This was done because Pharaoh feared that the Hebrews would outman, both in population and strength, the Egyptians. Therefore, Pharaoh sought to destroy the potential deliverers and warriors in their youth before they could reach maturity.

Understand, the enemy has not changed this tactic. The devil has been using the same strategies for eons of time. To this very day, the enemy attempts to drown our children in a sea of media, ungodly relationships, and confusion. We also see the plight of abortion that pervades our culture. Why? It is so he can destroy an arising generation and prevent them from reaching the fullness of their potential. Pharaoh was not frightened by the babies of Israel. Rather, he was afraid of potential revolution that could occur if those males were ever allowed to reach maturity. Satan is not necessarily scared of young people and young believers in their current level of spiritual maturity. Rather, the enemy sees future revolutionaries who are easier to target when they are small and weak.

Moses' mother, Jochebed, was intelligent and brave. She quickly acted and saved her son by putting him in a basket and covering him in the reeds by the riverbank. There is once again a spiritual modern parallel to the protection Moses' mother provided him in his infancy. God has raised up fathers and mothers, both natural and spiritual, to hide and protect potential revolutionaries who have yet to reach maturity. Their covering makes them impervious to the enemy being able to take them out. There is safety found in the covering of spiritual fathers and mothers! Thank God!

Moses was soon discovered by Pharaoh's daughter. This descendant of royalty came to bathe at the river. However, she went home with a baby that she then adopted and raised as her own. So, Moses grew in stature and wisdom while living in the house of the enemy.

The Seed of Revolution

If we fast-forward in the story, Moses was a strong man around forty years old, still abiding in the house of the enemy, Pharaoh. The future deliverer and leader of Israel had been raised as part of the Egyptian royal family. I would have to think he was afforded all the luxury that Egypt had to offer. Meanwhile, Moses' brethren were suffering under the sadistic crack of the whip of the taskmasters. The dichotomy between the lifestyle of Moses and the rest of the descendants of Abraham couldn't have been more stark. While Moses was afforded food, drink, and freedom, he heard the rattling of the chains in which his brethren were bound. However, all that was about to change in one single moment.

> Now it came to pass in those days, when Moses was grown, that he went out to his brethren and looked at their burdens. And he saw an Egyptian beating a Hebrew, one of his brethren. So he looked this way and that way, and when he saw no one, he killed the Egyptian and hid him in the sand (Exodus 2:11-12).

Upon seeing the suffering of his brethren, this man who was raised in the palace of Pharaoh had seen enough. Moses did not know this yet, but he was called to be a deliverer. Moses killed the taskmaster to save one Hebrew. I believe that we observe here the seed of revolution manifested prematurely.

However, there was a problem. What was that problem? The seed of revolution had not been to the place of encounter, the place of revival, the place of fire. Thus, it was insufficient to produce a lasting result. The next day, the one man that Moses saved was still going to be a slave. The only fruit brought forth from his action was one dead Egyptian.

God didn't want Moses to simply free one man from bondage. The plan of the Lord was for Moses to lead an entire nation out of bondage. It wasn't just one Egyptian that would be killed, but rather a great multitude of Egyptian soldiers and taskmasters would be drowned in the Red Sea (Exodus 14:1-31). The problem was simple, Moses was trying to operate as a revolutionary without first being in the place of revival. Therefore, he was ineffective.

Moses ended up fleeing from Egypt. He fled to the land of Midian. While sitting by a well, he encountered the daughters of Jethro. He eventually married one of Jethro's daughters, Zipporah. Moses and his wife had a son, Gershom, and he settled into a new life. Meanwhile, the desire for freedom and revolution waned inside of him. The normalcy of life began to set in. Moses settled for less than the manifestation of the seed with which he was born, the seed of revolution.

The greatest thing that will kill the seed of revolution is the trapping of normal and good. Nothing that Moses had was inherently bad, but he allowed it to momentarily distract him from his destiny. We can never allow the "good things" to keep us from pressing forward to see revolution manifested. Revolution was God's best for the life of Moses. No matter how good things were going for him, it didn't change the fact that his kin were still suffering in Egypt. No matter how good life may be going for you, never forget that there are many who are still suffering in bondage. The captives are waiting for you to manifest the fruit of revolution.

Unknowingly, Moses' normal life was about to be interrupted. The seed of revolution was going to meet the manifested fire of God. A total change in perspective would be brought forth in the life of Moses.

Fire Manifested

Before we continue with the narrative of Moses, I want you to realize that revival is typically characterized by fire. Jesus told the disciples that they would be baptized with the Holy Ghost and FIRE (Matthew 3:11). On the day of Pentecost there appeared to them divided tongues as of FIRE, and it sat upon those in the Upper Room (Acts 2:3). Whenever there is Holy Spirit revival that begins to break out, there is FIRE associated with His coming. Revival is encountering the presence of God, and God is described by the writer of Hebrews as a "consuming fire" (Hebrews 12:29). So, I find it particularly interesting what happens next in the life of Moses.

> Now Moses was tending the flock of Jethro his father-in-law, the priest of Midian. And he led the flock to the back of the desert, and came to Horeb, the mountain of God. And the Angel of the Lord appeared to him in a flame of fire from the midst of a bush. So he looked, and behold, the bush was burning with fire, but the bush was not consumed. Then Moses said, "I will now turn aside and see this great sight, why the bush does not burn." So when the Lord saw that he turned aside to look, God

> called to him from the midst of the bush and said, "Moses, Moses!" And he said, "Here I am." Then He said, "Do not draw near this place. Take your sandals off your feet, for the place where you stand is holy ground." Moreover He said, "I am the God of your father—the God of Abraham, the God of Isaac, and the God of Jacob." And Moses hid his face, for he was afraid to look upon God. And the Lord said: "I have surely seen the oppression of My people who are in Egypt, and have heard their cry because of their taskmasters, for I know their sorrows. So I have come down to deliver them out of the hand of the Egyptians, and to bring them up from that land to a good and large land, to a land flowing with milk and honey, to the place of the Canaanites and the Hittites and the Amorites and the Perizzites and the Hivites and the Jebusites. Now therefore, behold, the cry of the children of Israel has come to Me, and I have also seen the oppression with which the Egyptians oppress them. Come now, therefore, and I will send you to Pharaoh that you may bring My people, the children of Israel, out of Egypt" (Exodus 3:1-10).

Amid Moses' "normal" everyday life, the presence of God interrupted him. In the midst of tending flocks, God told Moses that he was called to more than just shepherding sheep. He communicated that there was divine purpose for his life. In essence, God called Moses to be a revolutionary.

Our Heavenly Father takes delight in divine interruptions. He desires to divinely interrupt our "normal" with His presence. Of course, how is His presence manifested? FIRE! It was this encounter with the fire that pushed Moses toward becoming the revolutionary he was always destined to be. When we have a real encounter with God's fire it begins to change everything about our normal mundane existence.

We need to once again see within the Church the manifestation of the fire of God. What do I mean when I say that? I am talking about the manifestation of His tangible presence. Revolutionaries are not born because they take a class on being a revolutionary. They are birthed out of the place of His presence. We have substituted religious programs for His presence. Therefore, we are not operating in reformation as the Church should be. The fire of God is what we need to bring forth revolutionaries.

Send the Fire

On July 2, 1865, a man named William Booth began a new organization called the Salvation Army. Today, the most that the majority know of this organization is that they stand outside of department stores around Christmas. Salvation Army volunteers stand and ring bells collecting donations for those who are less fortunate. While this is a noble endeavor, the Salvation Army was established upon much more than ringing bells and the collection of money.

The Salvation Army was founded as a force intent on bringing the gospel to all inhabitants in the earth. Booth and his wife, Catherine, in those early days began to reach alcoholics, prostitutes, and morphine addicts. These were people that were considered undesirable by many churches. The Salvation Army was revolutionary. In fact, Catherine Booth even preached. A woman preaching was relatively unheard of in that day; it was revolutionary. Of course, their ministry wasn't only in word, but also in deed. The Salvation Army helped to feed the hungry, provide for the poor, and many other social ministries.

Booth believed that all the world's problems could be solved by applying the Christian gospel and a good work ethic. As much as Booth believed in programs, he believed those programs had to be fueled by something: the fire of God. In 1894, William Booth wrote a song that became the anthem of the Salvation Army. The name of that song was "Send the Fire." Read the words of this powerful hymn. You can see how imperative Booth believed it was to encounter the fire of God.

Thou Christ of burning, cleansing flame,
Send the fire, send the fire, send the fire!
Thy blood-bought gift today we claim,
Send the fire, send the fire, send the fire!
Look down and see this waiting host,
Give us the promised Holy Ghost;
We want another Pentecost,
Send the fire, send the fire, send the fire!

God of Elijah, hear our cry:
Send the fire, send the fire, send the fire!
To make us fit to live or die,
Send the fire, send the fire, send the fire!
To burn up every trace of sin,
To bring the light and glory in,
The revolution now begin,
Send the fire, send the fire, send the fire!

'Tis fire we want, for fire we plead,
Send the fire, send the fire, send the fire!

The fire will meet our every need,
Send the fire, send the fire, send the fire!

For strength to ever do the right,
For grace to conquer in the fight,
For pow'r to walk the world in white,
Send the fire, send the fire, send the fire!

"Send the Fire" was first published in the Salvation Army publication, ***The War Cry*** in 1894. Its publishing marked the fiftieth anniversary of William Booth's conversion. I wholeheartedly believe this song was a prophetic declaration straight from heaven. This was more than a song; it was a prophetic decree of what God was preparing to do in the earth.

God anoints men and women to herald what He is preparing to do in the earth. We often call these heralds prophets. William Booth was one of these great prophets of God in the late nineteenth century. Prophetic declarations like the one Booth made in "Send the Fire" helped to usher in another Pentecost: the Azusa Street Revival. It was twelve years after this song was first published that the Azusa Street Revival began in California.

Let's break down some of the lines from "Send the Fire" and look at their importance to the subject as we expound on the fire of God.

"It's fire we want, for fire we plead."

We are living in a day where we must cry out for a visitation of the fire of God like never before. Fire is always sent on the other side of a group of people crying out for it. The fire did not fall by happenstance on the Day of Pentecost. No, there was a group of one hundred twenty souls in the upper room praying for it non-stop. If we want to see a fresh visitation of fire, let this cry of Booth's become ours once again.

Let's continue to look at the proclamations of Booth in this powerful hymn.

"The fire will meet our every need."

The Church needs to realize once again the simple fact that without the fire of God being manifested, we are absolutely nothing more than an assembly of people. The Church was birthed in fire and is sustained by fire (Acts 2). The fire meets every need we have. William Booth, who certainly believed in meeting material needs, realized that fire was of the utmost importance. No matter what we do in the natural, if it is lacking the visitation of His fire, it will always be lackluster and deficient. However, when we have the fire of God, it meets each and every need that we could ever possess.

The last lyrical line I want to point out is this,

"The revolution now begins."

When does the revolution begin? After the fire has been sent. Revolutionaries are birthed in fire. The reason we see a lack of true revolutionaries in our churches is due to a lack of fire. If we want to see revolutionaries birthed, we must cry out for fire. Moses, one of the greatest revolutionaries the world has ever known, was birthed from encountering the fire of God.

You Have the Goods

When encountering the fire of God in the bush at Mount Horeb, Moses received an impartation that enabled him to accomplish the revolutionary task that lay ahead. Not only will the fire empower us, it also takes away our excuses. Why? It is because once we have been given ability, there is no longer any excuse for not fulfilling your purpose and destiny.

During the events in chapters three and four of Exodus, Moses asked God several questions. He is making excuses and an answer emerges to every question. Where does the answer emanate from? The answer to every question came forth from the fire. The fire of God will meet every need that we ever encounter. William Booth truly had it right.

The other thing that is noteworthy is this fact: Moses already had access to everything he needed in his possession. Moreover, once those factors met fire, they were empowered in a new manner. We could say it this way, Moses had the goods. Check this out.

> Then Moses answered and said, "But suppose they will not believe me or listen to my voice; suppose they say, 'The Lord has not appeared to you.'" So the Lord said to him, "What is that in your hand?" He said, "A rod." And He said, "Cast it on the ground." So he cast it on the ground, and it became a serpent; and Moses fled from it. Then the Lord said to Moses, "Reach out your hand and take it by the tail" (and he reached out his hand and caught it, and it became a rod in his hand), "that they may believe that the Lord God of their fathers, the God

> of Abraham, the God of Isaac, and the God of Jacob, has appeared to you." Furthermore the Lord said to him, "Now put your hand in your bosom." And he put his hand in his bosom, and when he took it out, behold, his hand was leprous, like snow. And He said, "Put your hand in your bosom again." So he put his hand in his bosom again, and drew it out of his bosom, and behold, it was restored like his other flesh. "Then it will be, if they do not believe you, nor heed the message of the first sign, that they may believe the message of the latter sign. And it shall be, if they do not believe even these two signs, or listen to your voice, that you shall take water from the river and pour it on the dry land. The water which you take from the river will become blood on the dry land" (Exodus 4:1-9).

What is in our hand? That is the question we must ask ourselves as we read this. Realize we are not waiting for a special impartation to be a revolutionary. God has already given us everything we need to accomplish our destiny. The elements of our lives just need an encounter with the fire of His presence. God did not give Moses anything new in this encounter. He simply anointed and transformed what he already possessed. We have got the goods! God gave the tools to us, and His fire will transform them to instruments of revolution.

Additionally, God has already linked us with people who possess strength where we may be weak. Moses had a speech issue. He said that he was "slow of speech and slow of tongue" (Exodus 4:10). However, Aaron, the older brother of Moses, could speak well. So, Aaron was anointed as the spokesperson of Moses. Even in that, we see that God had already made a way for Moses in spite of his deficiency. God had already divinely orchestrated and set everything up. Moses' brother, a covenant relationship, was used for reformation and revolution. This was illuminated to him when he had an encounter with fire!

The sooner we realize that we already have everything we need for accomplishing our purpose, the sooner we can realize the fulfillment of our purpose. Remember this, "His divine power has given to us all things that pertain to life and godliness, through the knowledge of Him who called us by glory and virtue" (2 Peter 1:3). If He has given us all things, we have them. I know that seems simple, but realize we are not waiting for God to give us what we need. What we currently possess just needs an encounter with fire to be activated to reach the fullness of its potential.

From Fire to Revolution

Moses encountered God in a high place, on a mountaintop. However, his mountaintop encounter was always meant to lead him to something else. The mountaintop encounter was not the goal; the encounter was to activate Moses for a much greater purpose. Moses goes down the mountain to Egypt and ultimately leads one of the greatest revolutions the world has ever seen.

In a very short time, the Hebrews went from a place of slavery to a place of progressing toward promise. On top of that, the people of Egypt blessed them with silver, gold, livestock, and clothing on their way out (Exodus 12:35). Their oppressors began to bless them! The revolution Moses led wasn't merely spiritual. This revolution changed everything in the natural lives of the children of Israel as well. All of this was possible because of an encounter that Moses had with the fire of God.

Fresh Fire

We need to ask the Lord for a fresh encounter with His fire because the fire will meet every need. If we ask our Father for something, He is always faithful to deliver. God gives His children what they request by faith. Jesus said:

> Or what man is there among you who, if his son asks for bread, will give him a stone? Or if he asks for a fish, will he give him a serpent? If you then, being evil, know how to give good gifts to your children, how much more will your Father who is in heaven give good things to those who ask Him! (Matthew 7:9-11).

The fire of God is a good thing to request. Even more, it is a phenomenal thing to request! God will give it to us. We only need to ask.

I believe there is a fresh release of the manifest fire of God to transform men and women from those who tend flocks into revolutionaries who lead God's people from bondage to promise. Receive a fresh release and encounter with His fire today. As we do, the revolutionary call on our lives will begin to spring forth

CHAPTER 5

NO FEAR

> Paul, an apostle of Jesus Christ by the will of God, according to the promise of life which is in Christ Jesus, To Timothy, a beloved son: Grace, mercy, and peace from God the Father and Christ Jesus our Lord. I thank God, whom I serve with a pure conscience, as my forefathers did, as without ceasing I remember you in my prayers night and day, greatly desiring to see you, being mindful of your tears, that I may be filled with joy, when I call to remembrance the genuine faith that is in you, which dwelt first in your grandmother Lois and your mother Eunice, and I am persuaded is in you also. Therefore I remind you to stir up the gift of God which is in you through the laying on of my hands. For God has not given us a spirit of fear, but of power and of love and of a sound mind (2 Timothy 1:1-7).

Paul began his second letter to his spiritual son, Timothy, with a reminder of who he was called to be. He also exhorted him to stir up the gift that God had placed inside him. Paul continued to encourage and admonish Timothy to live free from intimidation and fear. Timothy was called as a revolutionary. Paul, a fellow revolutionary, realized that fear will always attempt to rear its ugly head in the lives of those with a strong assignment to perform a revolutionary work. Fear attempts to stop the spirit of revolution inside of Christians.

I believe that somewhere between the two letters Paul wrote to Timothy, something happened within the life of this young pastor. There was an event that caused him to sink back in expressing the destiny that God was desirous of him fulfilling. Timothy possibly had an encounter with rejection, disappointment, or even failure that produced fear in his life.

Therefore, Paul had to tell his spiritual son that he was not called to live a life of trepidation, worry, and fear. Timothy was admonished that fear did not belong in his life. Paul continued to exhort him with the declaration that he was given power, love, and a sound mind. Understand that as a revolutionary you must conquer one of the greatest enemies the devil uses: fear. Timothy had to conquer this foe, and so will we.

Simple Yet Powerful

I vividly remember a time where my wife and I went through a tough spot with our son, Josiah regarding him sleeping in his bed at night. Although it may seem trivial, it was incredibly frustrating to us. If you are a parent who has ever had a child who struggled with sleeping in their own bed, you understand.

Josiah frequently got up from his bed and came to our room in the middle of the night. Often, there would be tears streaming down his little cheeks. His reason for leaving his bedroom was that he was scared. He wasn't attempting to be dramatic; fear was attempting to attack him at a young age.

I remember a long period of time when I put him to bed and had him repeat 2 Timothy 1:7 before I left his room. When my son came to our room in the middle of the night, we returned him to his room and repeated 2 Timothy 1:7. I then asked, "Josiah, did God give you fear?" He responded through his tears, "No." I then asked, "What did God give you?" He finally responded in his high-pitched, gruff two-year-old voice, "God gave us power, love, and a sound mind." He quoted this while doing hand motions we had developed for this passage of Scripture.

After a season of time, Josiah stopped getting out of bed and had conquered the fear he had developed. I know that having the truth of 2 Timothy 1:7 imparted to his life was a tool used to get victory over fear and terror. The Word of God is powerful. Even in the life of a young two-year-old little boy, the Word of God was effective. Inside of His Word are tools to conquer anything and everything we may face in life.

While the Scripture in 2 Timothy can most certainly be used in the life of a child to help them overcome any type of fear or horror that they may be facing, this is a bit of an oversimplification of this Scripture. However, it is probably what this passage is used for most in Christianity. Most of us with Christian parents learned this Scripture at a young age when we encountered our first fear. However, there is so much more depth to this Scripture. Paul is not admonishing Timothy because he's scared of the dark, spiders, snakes, or any other sort of natural phobia. This is simply not the context of this Scripture at all. While this spiritual truth can certainly be appropriated for any natural fear, the declaration that Paul makes is so much deeper.

In this letter, Paul is encouraging Timothy to express the gifting God placed within him. The enemy cannot prohibit God from placing a gifting and an anointing in us, but he can cause us to live in fear and not express the gift which is there. Let's not reduce the power of this Scripture and thus miss the fullness of what this passage can mean in our lives. This Scripture is a weapon that once placed in the hands of revolutionaries becomes dominant over enemy forces of faintheartedness, terror, and trepidation.

The Effect of Fear

Everything that a revolutionary is called to do requires action. Therefore, if the enemy can provoke us to apathy and inactivity, our adversary has snuffed out the flames of revolution we are called to produce. You see, when a revolutionary begins to move in purpose and destiny, they can be likened to a runaway freight train; nothing can stop them. Therefore, what our enemy would like most is for us to never start. The methodology he uses to create his desired result is fear. Many members of our churches in this day and hour are bound by a spirit of fear that produces inactivity. Thus, we are not seeing the kingdom of God established in the manner that we as Christians are called to bring forth.

Incredibly, the presence of fear produces the manifestation of physical paralysis. A study from the University of Bristol released on April 23, 2014, discovered a chain of neural connections from the cerebellum. When these connections are initiated by a threat, real or imagined, these neural firings that are sent can literally cause the body to consequently freeze in terror. It doesn't even take an actual, factual, or credible threat to evoke this reaction. The threat must only be perceived.

Understand this, the enemy and his minions are of no real threat to revolutionaries. The devil's only real weapon is fear. Jesus has already defeated the enemy. Hallelujah! The victory of Jesus at the cross is now to be enforced by believers within the earth. So, the enemy will attempt to bring fear in the lives of Christians to paralyze them.

Intimidation through fear is the last-ditch effort of the enemy. The enemy masquerades as a credible threat to attempt to bring paralysis and stop the forward progression of revolutionaries. We must not fall prey to this desperate attempt of the enemy to impede the progress of our revolutionary work.

Lions have an astonishingly interesting tactic they use while hunting. They begin by stalking their intended prey, staying low and clandestine in order to get close enough to strike. Once they are close enough to begin their barrage, the last thing a lion will do before pouncing is roar. Why does the lion roar when it has taken such precautions to go undetected? The answer is very simple: to paralyze their victim.

Peter said that "your adversary the devil walks about like a roaring lion" (1 Peter 5:8-9). Peter points out an interesting fact about our adversary. Our enemy is not a roaring lion; the devil simply masquerades as one. So, while he may have the roar, our villainous foe has no teeth. If you realize he is toothless, his roar will not affect you. There is literally no reason to fear an enemy that has no bite. However, if we give him credit that he does not deserve, we become paralyzed by the roaring lies of the devil. We will live a life of inactivity, while territory we are called to seize goes unpossessed.

Fear Produces Wandering

In Numbers 13, we see the account of the children of Israel, fresh out of Egyptian bondage, begin to progress toward Canaan, their promised land. Upon their advance, God told Moses to send spies to check out the land that He had given them and return with a report of what they had scouted (Numbers 13:2).

Moses, being obedient to the voice of God, sent twelve spies, one from each tribe of Israel. The ones sent are: Shammua, from the tribe of Benjamin, Shaphat from the tribe of Simeon, Caleb from the tribe of Judah, Igal from the tribe of Issachar, Hoshea (Joshua) from the tribe of Ephraim, Palti from the tribe of Benjamin, Gaddiel from the tribe of Zebulun, Gaddi from the tribe of Manasseh, Ammiel from the tribe of Dan, Sethur from the tribe of Asher, Nahbi from the tribe of Naphtali, and Geuel from the tribe of Gad. Twelve choice men are selected.

I do not believe these men were selected because they had a propensity toward negativity or cowardice. On the contrary, these men were leaders with a desire to push forward and take the land that Moses had told them about. These men were probably leaders during the time of slavery in Egypt and continued in their roles of influence upon their exodus.

I think about the expectation that Moses held. The man who led the exodus most certainly had to expect a good report. After all, God told him that He was giving them the land. I believe Moses had a confident expectation of a positive report. Certainly, these twelve leaders were going to return with a glowing positive report. However, things did not go as Moses expected. Let's look at this:

> So they went up and spied out the land from the Wilderness of Zin as far as Rehob, near the entrance of Hamath. And they went up through the South and came to Hebron; Ahiman, Sheshai, and Talmai, the descendants of Anak, were there. (Now Hebron was built seven years before Zoan in Egypt.) Then they came to the Valley of Eshcol, and there cut down a branch with one cluster of grapes; they carried it between two of them on a pole. They also brought some of the pomegranates and figs. The place was called the Valley of Eshcol, because of the cluster which the men of Israel cut down there. And they returned from spying out the land after forty days. Now they departed and came back to Moses and Aaron and all the congregation of the children of Israel in the Wilderness of Paran, at Kadesh; they brought back word to them and to all the congregation, and showed them the fruit of the land. Then they told him, and said: "We went to the land where you sent us. It truly flows with milk and honey, and this is its fruit. Nevertheless the people who dwell in the land are strong; the cities are fortified and very large; moreover we saw the descendants of Anak there. The Amalekites dwell in the land of the South; the Hittites, the Jebusites, and the Amorites dwell in the mountains; and the Canaanites dwell by the sea and along the banks of the Jordan."

> And they gave the children of Israel a bad report of the land which they had spied out, saying, "The land through which we have gone as spies is a land that devours its inhabitants, and all the people whom we saw in it are men of great stature. There we saw the giants (the descendants of Anak came from the giants); and we were like grasshoppers in our own sight, and so we were in their sight" (Numbers 13:21-29, 32-33).

These selected choice men returned with an incredible negative report. Instead of speaking about taking the land, they pronounced that they would be devoured if they even attempted to enter the land. This was most probably like a kick in the gut for Moses. With an expectation to hear a good report, instead he heard a report of fear, doubt, and unbelief. This was followed by the Lord sentencing an entire generation of Hebrews to wander in the wilderness until they all died (Numbers 14:26-32). What was the root of the issue that caused this wandering to take place? It was fear! It was fear of the enemy, fear of the fight, fear of defeat, and fear of an unknown fate.

Inside church culture, we have frequently said that complaining kept the children of Israel out of the Promised Land. While this is true, the root of their complaining was based in fear. They complained against Moses because they feared the fight. They were scared of the consequences if they lost (Exodus 14:3). Every complaint and murmur was being fueled by a root of fear.

Think about it, these ten spies with a negative report had been partakers of one of the greatest revolutionary acts in history.

They had seen the plagues of Egypt, the Red Sea part, and ultimately that Red Sea collapse on Pharaoh and his army. However, amid all of this, they never dealt with a root of fear in their lives that developed while in the bondage of the Egyptian empire. If we don't deal with the root of fear, we will wander in the wilderness and God will raise up another to take what we were originally purposed to possess. Don't wander; reject fear.

Perspective of Proclaimers

Amid an overwhelming majority voicing fear, doubt, and unbelief, there arose two voices with a totally different perspective on what they had seen in Canaan. Joshua and Caleb had the perspective that revolutionaries must embrace, live with, and proclaim.

> But Joshua the son of Nun and Caleb the son of Jephunneh, who were among those who had spied out the land, tore their clothes; and they spoke to all the congregation of the children of Israel, saying: "The land we passed through to spy out is an exceedingly good land. If the Lord delights in us, then He will bring us into this land and give it to us, 'a land which flows with milk and honey.' Only do not rebel against the Lord, nor fear the people of the land, for they are our bread; their protection has departed from them, and the Lord is with us. Do not fear them" (Numbers 14:6-9).

Do not fear! What a proclamation that cut right to the root of the issue. There was something markedly different about what Joshua and Caleb declared. Contrasting this to what the other appointed spies had said to the congregation of Israel was remarkable. What made the difference? The spirit that rested upon them was what caused them to view things from a totally different perspective. This is illustrated later when God says this about Caleb:

> "My servant Caleb, because he has a different spirit in him and has followed Me fully, I will bring into the land where he went, and his descendants shall inherit it" (Numbers 14:24).

The word "spirit" used in Numbers 14 is from the Hebrew word *ruach*. If we study and look at an outline of biblical usage for this word, we find it can be defined as a *prophetic spirit*. The prophetic spirit that rested on Caleb enabled him to see beyond the perceived strength of the descendants of Anak. Caleb prophetically saw what God would do to the giants through his people, Israel. The plan of God was to bring destruction and devastation on the descendants of Anak. When Joshua and Caleb encountered the giants, they didn't see themselves devoured as the others did.

In the eyes of the other ten spies, they saw themselves as grasshoppers. Caleb and Joshua saw the children of Israel as conquerors. The great majority saw giants killing Hebrews. Caleb and Joshua saw dead giants defeated at the hands of God's people. These men of God realized that if God said they would have victory, then the giants would have no chance in battle. Joshua and Caleb realized that if God is for us, who can be against us (Romans 8:31)?

Let us stand with the same conviction and understanding as Joshua and Caleb. The greatest way to overcome fear is to realize that God is with us and on our side. Once we realize God is for us, we become fearless.

Because of fear, an entire generation died wandering in the wilderness. Moreover, Joshua and Caleb were the only people over twenty years old that were allowed to enter the Promised Land. What was the difference in their lives? Joshua and Caleb didn't allow themselves to be moved by fear. The size of the giant didn't frighten them. They realized the giant had yet to meet the power of their God.

Understand that as a revolutionary we will encounter giants standing in the way of our taking territory that God has called us to possess. The presence of spiritual giants merely reminds us we are on the right path. When we encounter these great enemies opposed to us, there is a simple decision to make. Will we allow fear to grip us and thus consign our fate to live a wandering life? The other option is to understand that the giant will come down if we aren't paralyzed by fear. We must make our choice today. We should choose to face down the giant. That is the revolutionary choice. It is the correct choice.

The Other Side

I have often thought about the fear that the revolutionaries and founding fathers must have faced whenever they began to stake their claim for independence in 1776. These men, who were largely not militaristic, were staring down a battle with the greatest fighting force the world had seen up until that point. There was nothing in the natural that would indicate that these farmers and militia men stood any chance of success and victory against the Redcoats. The revolutionaries had a choice to make. What would loom larger? Would it be their vision of a new nation or fear of defeat and the resulting losses?

I believe that one of the factors that contributed to men like Washington, Adams, and Franklin stepping out of the boat and embracing the revolution was a different spirit. These great men had a prophetic spirit, a *ruach*. They envisioned more than the battle. With prophetic foresight, these prodigious men could see beyond the impending struggle. These revolutionaries saw a nation established.

Fear attempts to get us to simply look at the struggle. The spies brought back a cluster of grapes that had to be carried on a pole with two men carrying each end (Numbers 13:23). That's a huge cluster of grapes unlike anything they had ever seen. For that matter, it is unlike anything that we see today. Moreover, they brought back figs and pomegranates (Numbers 13:23). The spies also witnessed that it was a land that flowed with milk and honey (Numbers 13:27).

However, they didn't focus on the fruit; they focused on the struggle. Sometimes we must look beyond the struggle and begin to see what is waiting on the other side. If they had focused more on the grapes, milk, and honey and less on the giants, then their fate would have probably been different. Assuredly, things would have happened other than four decades of wandering aimlessly to only die in the wilderness.

This still happens to this day, people don't focus on the fruit; they focus on the struggle. They look at the trajectory of an ungodly culture, and they see persecution. Thus, these elements cause them to be paralyzed in fear. Instead of focusing on the struggle, we should choose to look at the fruit.

What is the fruit awaiting those who embrace the revolutionary path? It is lives given to Jesus, marriages restored, universities experiencing revival, healing, signs, wonders, deliverance, and a turning of the tide of culture today. The fruit that is to be reaped is the world turned upside down. The fruit is greater than the obstacle.

President Theodore Roosevelt said, "Nothing in the world is worth having or worth doing unless it means effort, pain, difficulty." Understand, spiritually it is the same. No one has ever done anything revolutionary without facing down some giants. There will be opposition to anything of value done for Jesus and His kingdom. However, Christ has made you victorious.

There are two sides that you can choose to focus on. On side one there is the struggle, the difficulty that you are facing, and the size of the giant. On side two you can experience, the fruit, the glory of victory, and destiny fulfilled. Many who have been called to phenomenal things in the kingdom of God have not fulfilled their purpose because they focused on the former. They made a choice to live in fear. I choose to look at the other side. I refuse to live in fear. Why? It is because as long as I live in fear, I will never live in victory. In rejecting fear, I choose victory. Don't operate in fear and be paralyzed. Be a revolutionary. Choose victory.

CHAPTER 6

CAN'T STOP WON'T STOP

May 10, 1940, a sixty-five-year-old short, chubby man from Woodstock, England with a speech impediment who was considered an absolute political joke took office as the newly elected Prime Minister of England. Who was this oft ridiculed man? The man I am describing is Prime Minister Winston Churchill. There was probably never a direr time to assume the Prime Minister's office than the time in which Churchill assumed this responsibility and burden of leadership. The Nazi regiment, led by one of the worst dictators in all of history, Adolf Hitler, was advancing across Europe as World War II was ramping up in intensity. England was under threat of invasion from these ruthless forces. The future appeared bleak. Upon assuming residency in the Prime Minister's office at 10 Downing Street, under extremely perilous circumstances, Churchill made an address on public radio in which he said the following:

> We shall fight on the seas and oceans, we shall fight with growing confidence and growing strength in the air, we shall defend our island, whatever the cost may be, we shall fight on the beaches, we shall fight on the landing grounds, we shall fight in the

> fields and in the streets, we shall fight in the hills; we shall never surrender.

Complete and total defiance was the attitude that Churchill operated from when making this gutsy proclamation in the face of contrary circumstances. Regardless of the way that things may have appeared, Churchill refused to stop. The forces of England would continue to fight against the fascist Nazi forces. Churchill had made a determination of heart; we cannot stop and we will not stop until victory is realized. We will fight. We will persevere. We will not quit.

This is such a revolutionary attitude and spirit that is revealed in the heart of the phenomenal leader, Winston Churchill. Believers with the spirit and attitude of a revolutionary have a disposition that no matter what things may look like, no matter what may happen, no matter if culture looks hopeless, regardless of how many hate us, we have resigned deep within our spirits that we cannot stop, and we will not stop until we see victory in Jesus' name. We must understand that we cannot stop. Moreover, we will not stop. Surrender is not an option. We have resigned that we will keep fighting until victory is realized.

The Promise of Jesus: You Will Be Hated

You may have just read the heading that precedes this portion of the chapter and cringed. For that matter, you may have even rebuked me for writing such an anti-faith declaration. This is not a topic that we like to talk about in many modern church circles. However, it does not make it any less true. Jesus promised that those who are movers, shakers, and history-makers will be hated.

In the years that I have been in ministry, one of the things I have learned is there will always be people who hate you. There will always be people who oppose you. It doesn't matter what we do for Jesus. As a matter of fact, it is because of what we do for Jesus that there will always be a certain segment of people harboring contempt and abhorrence toward us. This is not negative faith; it is an inescapable fact. A fact that Jesus even promised. Look at what Jesus said when He commissioned and sent out the disciples:

> And when He had called His twelve disciples to Him, He gave them power over unclean spirits, to cast them out, and to heal all kinds of sickness and all kinds of disease..."And as you go, preach, saying, 'The kingdom of heaven is at hand.' Heal the sick, cleanse the lepers, raise the dead, cast out demons. Freely you have received, freely give. Provide neither gold nor silver nor copper in your money belts, nor bag for your journey, nor two tunics, nor sandals, nor staffs; for a worker is worthy of his food. Now whatever city or town you enter, inquire who in it is worthy, and stay there till you go out. And when you go into a household, greet it. If the household is worthy, let your peace come upon it. But if it is not worthy, let your peace return to you. And whoever will not receive you nor hear your words, when you depart from that house or city, shake off the dust from your feet. Assuredly, I say to you, it will be more tolerable for the land of Sodom and Gomorrah in the day of judgment than for that city! Behold, I send you out as sheep in the midst of wolves. Therefore be wise as serpents and harmless as doves. But beware of men, for they will deliver you up to

> councils and scourge you in their synagogues. You will be brought before governors and kings for My sake, as a testimony to them and to the Gentiles. But when they deliver you up, do not worry about how or what you should speak. For it will be given to you in that hour what you should speak; for it is not you who speak, but the Spirit of your Father who speaks in you. Now brother will deliver up brother to death, and a father his child; and children will rise up against parents and cause them to be put to death. And you will be hated by all for My name's sake. But he who endures to the end will be saved" (Matthew10:1, 7-22).

I know this passage can seem heavy and even somewhat contrary to what we have heard taught from many pulpits in our day. The idea of being hated is certainly contrary to our reasoning, emotions, and flesh. What Jesus says is certainly contrary to our desires. I don't want to discourage you, nor do I believe this is a discouraging passage of Scripture. If you can view this through the correct and proper lens, this passage will encourage you. Moreover, a proper perception will liberate you from seeking acceptance by man and release you to fulfill your purpose as a revolutionary force.

In this passage of Scripture, Jesus is sending His disciples out and commissioning them to walk in destiny and purpose. He tells them they are going to heal the sick, raise the dead, cleanse the leper, cast out demons, and have authority in the earth. Amen! Yes! Everyone loves that type of word of encouragement when it is released over their life. We shout and celebrate. We "feel the anointing" when we are recipients of this kind of commissioning and powerful proclamation over our purpose. We think to ourselves, "Yes, tell me how great I am. Come on Jesus, tell me about the glory and power I'm going to see released. I am in total agreement with this word."

Suddenly, without warning, Jesus shifts tone. "I send you out as sheep in the midst of wolves" (Matthew 10:16). We immediately begin to think, "Wait Jesus, I'm not so sure about that." Jesus continues, "But beware of men, for they will deliver you up to councils and scourge you in their synagogues" (Matthew 10:17). At this point, if this was being declared in a modern church, Jesus would be promptly removed from the pulpit and labeled a false prophet for having a victim mentality and releasing word curses over the lives of the saints of God.

However, Jesus is still not done. He says, "And you will be hated by all for My name's sake" (Matthew 10:22). In our post-modern church culture, most people have no capacity for criticism. Moreover, we certainly do not want to be hated. This is the point where many people begin rebuking the word being released. However, I have a news flash. It is impossible to successfully rebuke the words of the Word made flesh.

Jesus made us a guarantee: people will hate you. The sooner we can accept this fact, the sooner we can get about the business we are called to do. Understand this, His kingdom business will cause people to hate you. It really is simple to understand. If you cannot accept the fact that people will hate you, you will never fulfill God's purpose. If you are unable to handle hatred from the systems of this world, you will never be a spiritual revolutionary.

There is something inherent within man that desires to be adored, affirmed, and accepted. We dress a certain way to be popular. We talk in certain ways to be celebrated. We will do whatever we need to do to be prominent. No one likes to be hated. This is a simple fact. I have never met anyone who desires to be hated and reviled by men. Yet, that is exactly what Jesus promises. Jesus, the Prince of Peace, guaranteed that people would hate you.

Now, I know that our initial response to this is, "NO JESUS. I don't want to be hated." I know we respond in that manner because that is how my flesh feels as well. I want to be liked. I believe Paul totally understood that we would feel this way. For this very purpose, we are instructed to "mortify the deeds of the body" (Romans 8:13). Paul tells us that we must kill our flesh! Why? I propose that one rationale is because our flesh wants to be accepted and liked by everyone. Therefore, we must crucify our flesh and our desire to be loved by the multitudes. Unfortunately, no one has ever done anything significant for God while being loved and adored by the masses that are of the systems of the world. It is simply an impossible task.

We have such a desire to be liked and accepted, and to be culturally relevant that we praise megastar ministers when they are accepted in the inner-circles of the Hollywood elite. Many believers applaud these ministers who have successfully infiltrated areas that required compromise to arrive. While I certainly believe we are to reach those who are in a spiritually low place, we cannot compromise for the sake of acceptance (we'll talk about this in greater detail in a future chapter).

Many ministers have totally lost sight of the purpose of seeing transformation in hearts and lives. Why have they lost perspective? It's simple. They have fallen into the trap of wanting to be loved and accepted. At the root of this compromise is the fleshly desire for man's approval. The longing for everyone to love and accept them clouds their judgement. Lord liberate us from needing to have the approval of man.

The Trap of Acceptance

> Blessed are ye, when men shall hate you, and when they shall separate you from their company, and shall reproach you, and cast out your name as evil, for the Son of man's sake. Rejoice ye in that day, and leap for joy: for, behold, your reward is great in heaven: for in the like manner did their fathers unto the prophets...Woe unto you, when all men shall speak well of you, for so did their fathers to the false prophets (Luke 6:22-23, 26).

Jesus once again affirms in the Gospel of Luke that you are blessed when men hate you. Rejoicing and celebrating is not our normal response when we are reviled by people in culture. However, that is exactly the way we are commanded to respond by our Lord. Furthermore, Jesus draws a very interesting parallel between men speaking well of you and false prophets. Could it be that when we step into the place of seeking acceptance and striving for popularity that we begin to enter the danger zone and come perilously close to the place of false ministry? I certainly believe there is biblical precedent that in falling for the trap of seeking acceptance, we compromise our gifting, anointing, calling, and ultimately our very destiny and purpose.

We can look no further than Balaam to see the trap of being motivated by the fleshly ambition of wanting to be loved and accepted. It is totally irrefutable that Balaam was a false prophet. However, what made him a false prophet? Balaam most certainly heard from God and has a very accurate prophetic word. The Bible tells us in Numbers 23:5 that "God put a word in Balaam's mouth." Who put a word in Balaam's mouth? God did. God spoke to Balaam and caused him to declare what He was saying.

In our modern culture, we would call Balaam a true prophet based on this alone. Balaam even referred to the Lord as his God in Numbers 22:18. Think about this, Balaam could hear from heaven and furthermore declared Jehovah was God. So, it wasn't the ability to hear from God, the content of the prophetic word, or his confession toward the sovereignty of God in his life that made Balaam a false prophet.

What made Balaam a false prophet? It was his motivation. Balaam sought the favor, or we could say love and acceptance, of King Balak. Balaam attempted to improve his profile and reputation by getting cozy with Balak. Balaam was willing to compromise his gifting for position, praise, and profit. Those who had set themselves against God were the ones Balaam sought to appease. Balaam gave Balak advice that caused the Israelites to commit sin. This resulted in the anger of the Lord being aroused against Israel. This happened all because of the motivation of Balaam, not deficiency of anointing or gifting.

Peter writes in 2 Peter 2:15 that Balaam "loved the wages of unrighteousness." Balaam was motivated by acceptance and power, not the vision of the Lord. Let us not be those who fall for the trap of seeking acceptance, power, and notoriety, lest we cast our lot with Balaam. That is territory we should all avoid with everything within us.

Already Accepted

One reason many tend to fall for this trap of acceptance is because they are not fully settled with their acceptance in Christ. As a result, they strive to find fulfillment in places other than His affirmation and loving embrace.

One of the most important things for a revolutionary generation to do is get totally and completely settled in who they are in Christ Jesus. We were not created for the praise and acceptance of man. We were created to upset the proverbial apple cart. Revolutionaries don't blend into the masses. Revolutionaries turn the world upside down. Therefore, many seek their destruction and revile them. Just look at the early apostles and how they were found detestable by many.

Our destiny is not to be accepted by the world, its systems, and culture. Once we realize our acceptance in our Heavenly Father, His kingdom, and with His people, we will stop trying to be accepted by all of society and the elites of this present world. Revolutionaries can never and will never be accepted by the masses during the days of fulfilling their purpose.

The reality is the great masses don't understand or comprehend us. However, it is not our job to make them accept us. Our job is to be settled in our identity found in Christ and release freedom to the captives. We cannot accomplish this if we are still ourselves captive to the opinions of man.

The Place of Safety

While we have talked greatly over the last few pages about Jesus promising that we would be hated, Jesus didn't stop with those statements. Thankfully, He continued to speak. Jesus told us that "he that endures to the end will be saved" (Matthew 10:22). The first thing that Jesus stresses is the need for endurance. The Lord understood that when being faced with hatred and opposition we would require endurance and perseverance as a necessary character trait. We could say it this way: you must possess the quality of being so dedicated—so convinced of purpose—that you simply refuse to quit. We need a generation with that resolution today.

More importantly, I want to draw your attention to the fact that Jesus stated that those who endure will be saved! The word "saved" used in this context has nothing to do with being born-again. The Greek word used here is *sozo* which is defined as *to deliver or protect.* Jesus is actually referring to safety found in deliverance. It is so incredibly fascinating that after Jesus talks about being hated, scourged, and delivered to wolves that He talks about safety and deliverance. These thoughts almost seem antithetical by their very nature. However, these ideas are in perfect cohesion.

Jesus is emphasizing that when you operate with the mantle of a revolutionary, there will be some adverse situations you may stare down. However, your safety and deliverance are not found in stopping. Your place of safe harbor is found in continuing to do what you have been called to do.

The enemy will lie to us when we face difficulties and people bash us on social media with dishonest and fabricated stories.

He will tell us that if we stop, we will be safe. Nothing could be further from the truth. Our safety isn't found in abandoning our purpose and the passion God has birthed in us. Pressing forward is the only place safety is realized. If we stop, we become a sitting duck for the attack of the enemy. However, if we are willing to continue through difficulties and endure, there is safety. Our deliverance from the attack of the enemy is found in our commitment to never quit.

The Reason for Resistance

I find it so incredibly interesting that Jesus never talked about the disciples encountering this kind of resistance until one particular moment. What changed in their lives from the end of Matthew 9 to the beginning of Matthew 10? The answer is found in four simple words, "He gave them power..." (Matthew 10:1). The disciples are never promised this sort of response from man until they are given power by Jesus.

The word "power" that is used here is the Greek word *exousia* and it means *delegated influence—authority, jurisdiction, liberty, power, and strength*. Understand this fact, God has given His Church authority. Thus, people who may be motivated by principalities and powers will be stirred up with anger toward us. Why? It is because our actual authority is a challenge to the sham authority the enemy attempts to exercise.

Those who have been given *exousia* function in the earth as troublers (we'll talk about troublers in greater detail in an upcoming chapter). The fact that the power of God stirs up trouble is demonstrated in the life of Jesus. Check this out.

> Then they came to the other side of the sea, to the country of the Gadarenes. And when He had come out of the boat, immediately there met Him out of the tombs a man with an unclean spirit, who had his dwelling among the tombs; and no one could bind him, not even with chains, because he had often been bound with shackles and chains. And the chains had been pulled apart by him, and the shackles broken in pieces; neither could anyone tame him. And always, night and day, he was in the mountains and in the tombs, crying out and cutting himself with stones. When he saw Jesus from afar, he ran and worshiped Him. And he cried out with a loud voice and said, "What have I to do with You, Jesus, Son of the Most High God? I implore You by God that You do not torment me" (Mark 5:1-7).

Jesus is simply coming off a boat. He is not seeking some sort of confrontation. Yet, trouble seems to manifest in the life of Jesus through a man living in caves: the maniac of Gadara. In the middle of Jesus having a normal day (at least as normal a day as Jesus could have), He is interrupted by this man.

His cry to Jesus of "do not torment me" is fascinating. There is nothing indicating that Jesus was seeking this man out. Certainly, Jesus meant no harm to him. This demoniac came to Jesus; Jesus didn't go to him. Why? It was because the anointing, power, and influence that was upon the life of Jesus stirred up trouble with those under the influence of the enemy. You must understand that there are times the anointing on your life will cause people nearby to act in strange and peculiar ways for seemingly no reason at all.

My Encounter with a Maniac

I have had many encounters throughout my life with people being motivated by demonic powers of the enemy. However, there is one that sticks out to me because it was so bizarre.

Recently, my family and I took a vacation. After being head-long in the process of planting a church in the greater Orlando area, which involved uprooting and moving our family, we needed to take a break. At the time we took this vacation, our daughter, Hannalee Hope, was three years old. One night while we were at dinner there was a live band and a dance floor that was open for anyone to access. As a little girl who had taken ballet lessons the year before, Hannalee begged to go dance. As a father who loves his little girl, I of course said, "Yes." I accompanied Hannalee to the dance floor and danced with her. This was the type of moment with my daughter that I had hoped would be a positive life-long memory. The floor had several couples dancing and at least a dozen kids of varying ages dancing as well.

While my daughter was dancing, I was approached by a man who had to be in his sixties and his dance partner. This gentleman asked me if that little girl was my daughter while indicating he was talking about Hannalee. I politely responded, "Yes sir," fully expecting him to remark on how cute she is while doing her pointing and plies'. This man proceeds to get in my face and implore me to remove Hannalee from the dance floor. He is very adamant that, "Kids have their play-grounds; this is my playground." I was shocked and honestly didn't even know how to respond. I kind of chuckled because I was sure he had to be joking, and I had no idea how to respond as I was caught off-guard.

I look around and saw at least a dozen kids, and yet he singled my daughter out. There was not a word said to another child or parent. I was totally and completely perplexed. There were other children being much more rambunctious and wild than Hannalee. Why target us?

Now, I am not someone who likes confrontation, so I attempted to just steer my daughter clear of this angry and delusional man. He continued to press the issue with me time and time again. The man was becoming more aggressive with each passing moment for no apparent reason. Finally, this unhinged man looked at me and said, "You need to remove her. I would hate it if she accidentally was hurt if I happened to run her over."

At this point, my blood was boiling. No matter how rude, it was one thing to make this request, it was something completely different to make a veiled threat as a sixty-year-old man against an innocent three-year-old little girl who was just trying to have fun with her daddy on vacation. I simply responded at this point with a very firm, "She's fine, bro. She's a little girl having fun on vacation. Chill out!" Hannalee finished her dance without incident and we returned to our table to complete dinner.

This entire incident was very upsetting to me. I could hardly touch my food I had ordered for dinner because I was so upset. Out of all the people on that dance floor, something within him caused him to single out and target me and my three-year-old daughter for his onslaught. As I continued to think about what the possible reason for this outburst could have been, it finally hit me around noon the next day.

There could only be one real and logical answer. Whenever you are operating in an anointing, people who are of the culture of the world will be provoked for no logical reason at all. I had encountered resistance for no real reason other than, I believe, the anointing and calling on my life. I don't say that in some sort of braggadocios manner, but rather to reveal the resistance that we can face in insignificant moments for seemingly no logical reason at all.

I was simply on vacation when I had this experience. I wasn't preaching, prophesying, or evangelizing. I wasn't even wearing any sort of Christian apparel. However, I encountered this absurd resistance from an elderly man. There was a choice to make. Would I allow this road block to prevent me from having fun with my family? The answer to this question was a resounding "NO!" I became even more determined to have fun.

Likewise, when we encounter people who confront us, single us out, and even threaten us, we cannot let it stop us from pursuing our purpose and destiny. There will always be crazy people who appear threatening and are loud in their disapproval of us. Let's see how Jesus handled this with the maniac of Gadara.

Stay the Course

> For He said to him, "Come out of the man, unclean spirit!" Then He asked him, "What is your name?" And he answered, saying, "My name is Legion; for we are many." Also he begged Him earnestly that He would not send them out of the country. Now a large herd of swine was feeding there near the mountains. So all the demons begged Him, saying,

> "Send us to the swine, that we may enter them." And at once Jesus gave them permission. Then the unclean spirits went out and entered the swine (there were about two thousand); and the herd ran violently down the steep place into the sea, and drowned in the sea. So those who fed the swine fled, and they told it in the city and in the country. And they went out to see what it was that had happened. Then they came to Jesus, and saw the one who had been demon-possessed and had the legion, sitting and clothed and in his right mind (Mark 5:8-15).

Jesus was in no manner swayed or bothered by the intimidating appearance or behavior of this demon possessed man. Jesus kept doing what the anointing on His life demanded: bring freedom to the captives. We are told in the Bible, "For this purpose the Son of God was manifested, that He might destroy the works of the devil" (1 John 3:8). Jesus didn't come to earth to win a popularity contest. He came to destroy the works and bondages of the enemy. So, when this maniac showed up, Jesus was not bothered. No, Jesus didn't even slow down. Jesus did what He was called to do. Jesus ministered freedom and loosed the hold of the enemy on the life of this Gadarene man.

Keep Moving

I can guarantee you that when you embrace the mantle of a revolutionary you will encounter your fair share of proverbial maniacs of Gadara. You will encounter some resistance. You must make a choice to not let their appearance, threats, or vile hatred affect you. Simply continue to act in the manner you are called to behave. We must not be swayed from releasing revolution in the earth. There's an old adage that says, "When the going gets tough, the tough get going." I'd like to update that for our purposes and say, **"When the calling of God gets tough, revolutionaries keep going."**

Remember, the greater the resistance, the greater the victory will be. Thomas Paine, one of the most influential founding fathers of the United States, wrote a significant pamphlet entitled ***The American Crisis***. In this pamphlet, Paine brilliantly articulated this very point. This powerful pamphlet was published in December of 1776, just a few months after the signing of the Declaration of Independence.

Thomas Paine understood that the battle against the army of Great Britain would not be easy. The American struggle for Independence had encountered numerous setbacks in its infancy. The reality is that the outlook was dire for the American Revolution. General Washington and his troops had suffered humiliating defeats and even lost New York City (one of the key strategic cities for America) to British troops. Between September and December, over eleven thousand American volunteers gave up the fight and returned to their families. Things were certainly not going the way the American founding fathers had envisioned.

Paine wrote ***The American Crisis*** pamphlet as an encouragement in a time where many were greatly discouraged. General George Washington had this pamphlet that Paine wrote read to the men he was leading when they were encamped at McKonkey's Ferry on the Delaware River opposite Trenton, New Jersey. These farmers turned soldiers were facing cold, starvation, and a strong militant force. The

American revolutionaries were facing perilous conditions to say the least. Washington had the following words written by Thomas Paine in ***The American Crisis*** read aloud to his men:

> These are the times that try men's souls. The summer soldier and the sunshine patriot will, in this crisis, shrink from the service of their country; but he that stands by it now, deserves the love and thanks of man and woman. Tyranny, like hell, is not easily conquered; yet we have this consolation with us, that the harder the conflict, the more glorious the triumph.

Thomas Paine understood that pursuing the revolutionary life would be difficult and hazardous at times. However, the victory experienced was worth every ounce of adversity that might be encountered. After General Washington had these powerful words read to his men, they crossed the Delaware River, won the Battle of Trenton, and subsequently the Battle of Princeton. Momentum had shifted in the battle for American independence. Why? It was because they made a choice. General Washington and the American revolutionaries refused to quit. They made a choice to keep going. They continued to pursue even when it was difficult.

We must make a choice to stay the course of fulfilling our purpose as revolutionaries regardless of the posturing of people we may encounter. Why? It is because our safety is found in the fact that we WILL NOT STOP and CANNOT STOP! No matter what may be thrown at us, we will not stop. No matter what others may call us, we cannot stop! We are persuaded of our purpose and refuse to quit until we see breakthrough.

Revolutionaries have accepted the fact that they will probably not be loved by everyone. That is okay. Our fulfillment is found in releasing revolution, not being praised by the masses. Refuse to be the "sunshine patriot" or the "summer soldier" that Thomas Paine talked about. Don't be one who quits when the going gets tough. Stand your ground. Continue to fight and pursue victory. Keep moving toward your destiny. You are called to be a revolutionary!

CHAPTER 7

TROUBLERS

I want to begin this chapter by talking about a very significant event in history, the Boston Tea Party. For even the most cursory student of American history, just mentioning this event begins to stir up patriotism and visions of revolutionaries dumping tea into the Boston Harbor. This was an inconceivable activity for this group of colonists to engage. This wasn't just light petty vandalism; this was an act of defiance to the strongest empire in the world during that colonial era.

Why did the revolutionaries dump tea in the Boston Harbor? It was a direct result of the Tea Act of 1773. While the Townshend Revenue Act of 1767 created a tax on tea, the Tea Act of 1773 granted the British East India Tea Company a monopoly on tea sales in the American colonies. No other company was lawfully permitted to import or sell tea. Ultimately this was the culmination of a plethora of what were perceived as unjust rulings from the Crown of England in relation to the American colonies. The relationship between King George, Parliament, and the American colonists had reached a tipping point.

In response to these decrees from the mother country, on December 16, 1773, the Sons of Liberty disguised themselves as Mohawk Indians, boarded three ships moored in the harbor, and proceeded to dump 92,000 pounds of tea directly into the Boston Harbor. That amount of tea would have been able to yield approximately 18,400,000 cups of tea. That is a huge amount of tea. Economists and historians believe the amount of damage done by this act is the modern equivalent of $1,200,000. That is a significant amount of money.

This act of revolutionary defiance troubled King George and all of England. Ultimately, this caused an escalation of tensions and is viewed as a major catalyst for the coming American Revolution. We must understand, the Sons of Liberty were merely behaving in the appropriate manner of a revolutionary group of men. These men were creating trouble for the unjust rulers of the day. People with a revolutionary spirit will always revolt and rebel against unjust oppression in their time. Likewise, spiritual revolutionaries will stir up trouble for powers that set themselves against God to bring unrighteousness in the world. Being one who causes trouble for ungodly leaders is simply in the DNA of both natural and spiritual revolutionaries.

The Troubler of Israel

Elijah has always been a favorite biblical figure of mine. His story and relationship with Elisha was one of the primary focuses of my book ***Sonship: The Mantle. The Journey. The Double Portion.*** The character and ministry of Elijah is indicative of what a true prophet of God and revolutionary should look like. Elijah was bold and anointed, and he knew what his mission was to accomplish. Moreover, Elijah had a reputation with those who stood opposed to what was godly and righteous. These antagonists of all that was holy called Elijah a "troubler." Let's look at an account between the evil King Ahab and Elijah.

> Then it happened, when Ahab saw Elijah, that Ahab said to him, "Is that you, O troubler of Israel?" And he answered, "I have not troubled Israel, but you and your father's house have, in that you have forsaken the commandments of the Lord and have followed the Baals. Now therefore, send and gather all Israel to me on Mount Carmel, the four hundred and fifty prophets of Baal, and the four hundred prophets of Asherah, who eat at Jezebel's table" (1 Kings 18:17-19).

Elijah was identified in a derogatory manner as a troubler of Israel. What Ahab really meant was that the prophet Elijah opposed him. Ahab was quite annoyed by this opposition. What Ahab really meant was the man of God would not bow to his system of ungodly rule. What Ahab really meant was that this "troubler" was creating problems for him and his tyrannical reign.

Ahab had at least four hundred prophets who would simply agree with him. These men would tell him whatever he wanted to hear (1 Kings 22:6). These prophets did nothing more than tickle the ears of the king. They did not release the heart, mind, and will of God as true prophets are called, ordained, and commanded. I am of the persuasion that these men were originally called to be voices of truth, but somewhere along the line they began to compromise their original intent, design, and purpose.

Why would these men compromise? It is quite simple. They wanted favor with the cultural leaders of the day, King Ahab and Queen Jezebel. How many prophets do we have today that are willing to compromise their message and morals to gain favor within society and culture? I would rather preach, prophesy, and declare truth while being hated by the prevailing figures in culture than compromise. Compromise will cause us to comp (give away) our promise. Compromise will lead to the forfeiting of true destiny and identity.

Suddenly, there arose a prophetic voice who was countering the ungodly and reprehensible King Ahab. Elijah seemingly showed up in the biblical narrative out of nowhere. Why would this happen? Let me propose something. Could it be that God accelerated Elijah and put him at the forefront because He needed someone to counter Ahab and Jezebel's wickedness? I believe that was a very probable and likely reason.

All the previous kings of Israel combined did less to enrage God than Ahab in his reign (1 Kings 16:33). The voice of Elijah was given a platform of influence simply because Elijah was one who was willing to say, "Yes. Here I am, send me." He was willing to boldly speak what God was saying. Furthermore, Elijah was not concerned about pleasing man, but rather pleasing God. I believe the Lord is preparing to accelerate the callings, ministries, and ministry platforms of revolutionaries who are willing to say, "Yes. Here I am, send me." He is preparing those who will speak the truth, and not compromise in the face of our corrupt culture.

Elijah, as a true prophet of God, refused to comply and join with the ungodly system of Ahab and Jezebel. When they attempted to accomplish something wicked, there was Elijah standing in the way. This man of God was constantly telling them that God will not stand for their ungodliness. When most voices in the land are standing in acceptance of unholy behavior, being a voice of truth can seem offensive and like an affront to the order of the day.

Those from the order of the kingdom of God will always clash with those who are from the order of the kingdoms of this world. It is simply unavoidable. There will always be a clash between the way of the Lord and the way of the world.

Imagine if Elijah was alive today as part of the post-modern American church. What if he was living in a church culture where we were concerned about being liked and finding approval from those in the culture of the world? If that were the case, Elijah would probably be told he wasn't very Christ-like by many social media theologians. Elijah would probably be called a fault-finding negative prophet who doesn't really understand the nature of God's love. After all, challenging people to a showdown is not acting as a peacemaker; it is seemingly the opposite of seeking peace.

Remember, Jesus said in the Sermon on the Mount, "Blessed are the peacemakers, for they shall be called the sons of God" (Matthew 5:9). How can Elijah be a prophet of God, let alone a son of God, while doing something that seems so anti-peacemaker? Many today would proclaim, "Elijah just needs to understand God's love and then he won't be so confrontational and angry." Could it be possible that we have misunderstood what Jesus was communicating in the Sermon on the Mount? Are we viewing it from our modern Western perspective and missing the truth of the point? Let's look and find the answer.

Confrontational Peacemakers

When Jesus talked about being peacemakers in the Sermon on the Mount, He was not speaking of being passive in nature and never confronting culture. If that was the case, Jesus wouldn't qualify as a peacemaker. Remember, He was continually confronting culture in His day. He called the Scribes and Pharisees a "brood of vipers" (Matthew 23:33). The men who were the religious and political leaders of the day were being referred to by sweet and loving Jesus as snakes!

Paul, who next to Jesus, was the most influential figure in shaping Christendom, went and preached in Athens, Greece. Athens was the epicenter of arts and culture in that era. Famous philosophers such as Epicurus (Epicureanism) and Zeno (Stoicism), had lectured and taught in Athens. Suddenly, Paul arrived preaching and confronting the hotbed of culture, arts, and intellectualism. The apostle Paul, on this trip to Athens, confronted and preached truth to the leading philosophers. Paul spared no punches. He told them they had been worshipping false gods, informed them they had operated in ignorance (the greatest insult to the academic elite), and implored them to repent. This message by Paul was confrontational in nature.

Defining a True Peacemaker

The Greek word for "peacemaker" used in the Sermon on the Mount has two root words meaning t*o make the way that leads to peace and salvation.* This is a little different than what many perceive when they read the word peacemaker at a surface level. The word Jesus used that we translate as peacemaker is not referring to being agreeable at the cost of forfeiting what is right.

In no way is Jesus communicating that the person who sits back and keeps their mouth shut about sin is going to be blessed. We cannot sit back and watch society proceed as a runaway train on the highway to hell—willing to compromise, and continuing to "evolve on the issues." These people are not going to be blessed. These people will not be blessed because they are not peacemakers. Peacemakers are those who make the way for true peace and salvation to be realized. Sometimes peace only comes through confrontation of what is bringing discord and destruction into society.

I want to make sure you realize the following point: those who are revolutionaries don't simply have a "pow-wow" with demonic powers that are motivating people to act, behave, and govern in an unrighteous manner. Revolutionaries confront them and war in the heavenlies through their intercession, worship, and prophetic decrees. We can no longer afford to sit back and observe our world slide into moral decay because we feel we need to be "peacemakers." We must be true peacemakers and war against that which stands opposed to the moving of God in the earth. If we don't, who will?

Once again, if Jesus was declaring that being a peacemaker was about conforming and remaining mute when it comes to controversial issues, Jesus was a miserable failure as a peacemaker. After all, it was Jesus who said, "Do not think that I came to bring peace on earth. I did not come to bring peace but a sword" (Matthew 10:34). Contrary to what you may have heard, Jesus came to start a fight. The birth of Jesus in the earth was an announcement of war. Yes, the angels proclaimed, "On earth peace, goodwill toward men" (Luke 2:14). However, we must understand that this announcement of peace toward man was equally an announcement of war against the enemy. It was the first shot fired in the final battle of seeing man liberated from sin and death.

An act releasing peace toward one group was also an act of war against another group. Jesus' coming was an act of love and peace toward us while the coming of Christ was equally an act of aggression and war toward satan, his sham kingdom, sin, death, and the grave.

Prophets release words that are peaceful and life-giving to the people of God. However, these words are often in defiance to the culture of the world and the kingdom of darkness. The days of the Church going with "the flow" in order to be "peacemakers" is over. Troublers are arising within the earth this very hour.

Don't Be a Brawler

I would like to bring some balance to the idea of being confrontational. I believe that prophets are called to confront. However, I have met some men and women who are angry, rude, and derogatory toward anyone other than themselves, all the while calling this prophetic. If a person believes they are the only person doing anything of worth for Jesus and His Kingdom, they have entered the danger zone.

People who behave in this manner, constantly berating someone, especially other Christians and ministers of the gospel, are operating in a critical spirit. We will find that these men and women often are silent on the true issues of sin, ungodliness, and unrighteous behavior that plague society. Instead of addressing real issues of consequence, they would rather quarrel over style of ministry than address substantive issues facing the world.

Many who have a prophetic calling, if not vigilant, can cross over into the error of operating from a critical spirit. No one likes a brawler—one who is always looking for a fight. While we should certainly be bold and even confrontational, we can be bold without being aggressive and rude toward fellow brothers and sisters in Christ. Speak the truth, but never neglect love. To put it simply, don't be a jerk. *Selah.*

Stop Straddling

We must understand that as a revolutionary generation arises in the earth, the days of straddling the fence are coming to an end. We can no longer be those who are comfortable to worship in church and then compromise in the work place. We can no longer publicly extol the greatness of God while privately living a life that is antithetical to His standards.

Not to be crass, but naturally speaking, straddling the fence is an uncomfortable position to assume. If you straddle a fence it is going to produce nothing but pain. I believe spiritually this is also true. If you straddle the fence of the kingdom of God and the kingdom of man, it will ultimately produce nothing but pain. There is an uncomfortable feeling that is going to happen in the lives of those who have been straddling the fence. This feeling will provoke a choice to be made.

I believe in this hour God is drawing a line in the sand and He is saying, "Choose your side." We can no longer prophesy and seek acceptance found in the arms of pop culture. There are far too many preachers who are seeking an invitation to a daytime talk-show rather than seeking to be a revolutionary. While I don't doubt these men and women love Jesus, they are seeking affirmation from an incorrect source. It is a virtual impossibility to make a lasting revolutionary impact and be praised by man. We must accept that being a revolutionary means that we are setting ourselves against today's systems. We cannot be a friend of God and a friend of the world and its culture. Look at what James said.

> Adulterers and adulteresses! Do you not know that friendship with the world is enmity with God? Whoever therefore wants to be a friend of the world makes himself an enemy of God. Or do you think that the Scripture says in vain, "The Spirit who dwells in us yearns jealously"? (James 4:4-5).

James is very clear in this passage. We must choose a side. We cannot have it both ways. Would you rather be popular with man or make an impact?

There came a day in colonial America when they had to make a choice. Would they remain subservient and gain favor with the king, or would they pursue the dream of freedom, liberty, and independence? The colonists knew that pursuing freedom would mean they may lose friends, family, and even their reputation. However, they knew what they were called to do and that any loss was worth gaining independence and freedom.

It is impossible to befriend the world and fulfill our purpose. We are either a part of the revolutionary force of the kingdom of God, or we are of the world. We are either one who is part of the culture of the world, or we are a trouble-maker to the kingdom of darkness. I want to be a trouble-maker. I want it to be that when the enemy sees me coming he exclaims, "Here comes trouble!"

You Just Made the List

I believe that the forces of hell have a running list of those who are viewed as threats to their perceived dominion, a watch-list of troublers if you will. It goes without saying that I want to be known by our Heavenly Father, but I also want to be known by our enemy. It is a pursuit of my life to be on the watch-list of the enemy. I want to have a reputation with him. Jesus obviously had a reputation with the enemy, as did Paul. Check this out:

> Now God worked unusual miracles by the hands of Paul, so that even handkerchiefs or aprons were brought from his body to the sick, and the diseases left them and the evil spirits went out of them. Then some of the itinerant Jewish exorcists took it upon themselves to call the name of the Lord Jesus over those who had evil spirits, saying, "We exorcise you by the Jesus whom Paul preaches." Also, there were seven sons of Sceva, a Jewish chief priest, who did so. And the evil spirit answered and said, "Jesus I know, and Paul I know; but who are you?" Then the man in whom the evil spirit was leaped on them, overpowered them, and prevailed against them, so that they fled out of that house naked and wounded (Acts 19:11-16).

Paul is the picture of a man who decided he would rather be right in the sight of God than right with culture. I imagine that when Saul was converted and changed his name to Paul (an identity change), that he lost friends, family, and colleagues. Moreover, it is probable that many of the ones who worked with him to execute Christians were now attempting to kill him for becoming a Christian. Despite what he lost, Paul still chose to be a troubler and revolutionary. Because Paul bought-in to what God had called him to do, he had unusual miracles. Paul was a revolutionary in every sense of the word.

So, a group of religious leaders, Jewish exorcists, saw Paul and the fruit he was having in the supernatural realm and decided to mimic his ministry style. The problem is that these men were more interested in social acceptance than being revolutionary. They looked at ministry to further their popularity rather than to influence, change, and shift culture. Paul had *dunamis* power given by the Holy Spirit because of his relationship with Christ. The exorcists lacked this authority and power. So, these seven sons of Sceva decided to mimic Paul to try to get the same results and further their notoriety.

The spirits these Jewish exorcists attempted to cast out made an interesting statement. They said, "Jesus I know, and Paul I know; but who are you?" (Acts 19:15) Wow. It certainly could be argued that there is some sort of list being kept that includes people of whom the enemy is afraid. They didn't just say they knew Jesus, but they also knew Paul. The evil spirits knew Jesus. The Savior caused trouble for them and He was on their list. The spirits knew Paul. He was causing trouble for them everywhere he set his foot. Paul was on their list.

There are a lot of believers today who have not made the list. They are merely interested in performing a spectacle for the sake of promoting their own kingdom and propping themselves up. These people are no different than the seven sons of Sceva. Let it not be said of us that we want to move in miracles, but also be accepted by society. I want to make the watch-list of the enemy. I want to be a troubler just like Elijah, Jesus, and Paul.

Showdown Time

When troublers meet the systems of culture, it always ends in a showdown. That's exactly what happened with Elijah. The great troubler, this prophet, was going to have a showdown on Mount Carmel with 850 false prophets. From a natural perspective, the odds don't appear to ever be in favor of the prophet of God. He is outnumbered by a huge margin. However, as the Bible says, if God is for us who can be against us (Romans 8:31).

I've often thought about how giddy Ahab must have been knowing he had such a numbers advantage. God was simply setting up things to display and show His power. It may appear that the systems of the world outnumber the people of God, but our Father is preparing to show out in a big way. When God does something, He does it big.

On the top of that mountain, Elijah revealed how this showdown was going to work; he said, "Take two bulls, slaughter them, cut them in pieces, lay them on the altar, but put no fire underneath them." Elijah said, "You call on the name of your gods, and I will call on the name of the Lord; and the God who answers by fire, He is God" (1 Kings 18:24).

The prophets of Baal went first and spent hours crying out and dancing around the altar. However, there was no voice, no fire, and no answer. Elijah then began to mock them. It certainly appeared that the troubler was just having fun and entertaining himself at that point. Elijah said to the false prophets: "Cry aloud, for he is a god; either he is meditating, or he is busy, or he is on a journey, or perhaps he is sleeping and must be awakened" (1 Kings 18:27). Elijah was openly mocking the prophets of Baal. The false prophets then began to cut themselves and cry out for several more hours. Still there was no voice, no fire, and no answer. The prophets of Baal finally relinquished their efforts having failed.

Look at what happened when Elijah took his shot:

> Then Elijah said to all the people, "Come near to me." So all the people came near to him. And he repaired the altar of the Lord that was broken down. And Elijah took twelve stones, according to the number of the tribes of the sons of Jacob, to whom the word of the Lord had come, saying, "Israel shall be your name." Then with the stones he built an altar in the name of the Lord; and he made a trench around the altar large enough to hold two seahs of seed. And he put the wood in order, cut the bull in pieces, and laid it on the wood, and said, "Fill four waterpots with water, and pour it on the burnt sacrifice and on the wood." Then he said, "Do it a second time," and they did it a second time; and he said, "Do it a third time," and they did it a third time. So the water ran all around the altar; and he also filled the trench with water. And it came to pass, at the time of the offering of the evening sacrifice, that Elijah the prophet came near and said, "Lord God of Abraham, Isaac, and Israel, let it

> be known this day that You are God in Israel and I am Your servant, and that I have done all these things at Your word. Hear me, O Lord, hear me, that this people may know that You are the Lord God, and that You have turned their hearts back to You again." Then the fire of the Lord fell and consumed the burnt sacrifice, and the wood and the stones and the dust, and it licked up the water that was in the trench. Now when all the people saw it, they fell on their faces; and they said, "The Lord, He is God! The Lord, He is God!" And Elijah said to them, "Seize the prophets of Baal! Do not let one of them escape!" So they seized them; and Elijah brought them down to the Brook Kishon and executed them there (1 Kings 18:30-40).

God showed up and answered by fire when the troubler called on His name. The same is still true today. God will answer by sending His fire when those who society has labeled as troublers begin to call upon Him. The prophet Elijah was not content to merely watch as Ahab, Jezebel, and their minions seized control of what belonged to God. Neither should we be content to sit back and watch immorality and unrighteousness rule in our day. David said, "The earth is the Lord's, and all its fullness" (Psalm 24:1). It's time we arise as troublers, see God answer our call by fire, and see the destruction of spiritual enemies who have set themselves against God's kingdom.

Confrontation Brings Repentance and Restoration

The other effect that transpires as God answers the calls of a troubler is that those who are around to witness the fire of God begin to worship Jehovah as the true God. I have heard many argue that if we are confrontational it will turn people away from God. Obviously, Elijah did not receive this memo. The exact opposite was true. Israel had become wrapped up and overrun by worship of Baal, until Elijah showed up and confronted what was wrong. If Elijah had not possessed enough fortitude to confront ungodliness, these people may never have worshipped God as the one true God. Confrontation doesn't turn people away from God, it makes way for God to reveal the magnitude of His power to those who are far from Him. It's time to shift our thinking and no longer be afraid to confront ungodliness in our society.

I believe as we arise as troublers, do exploits, and confront the systems of the enemy that many are going to have their eyes opened and will worship Jehovah as the one true God! Let the troublers arise! Let the revolutionaries come forth!

CHAPTER 8

COME OUT OF THE CAVE

Saturday, June 26, 2015, is a day that will forever be emblazoned within my memory. I can recall it like it was just yesterday. It was a typical hot and humid summer day in central Florida. On this day, I was spending time with my family and preparing for our upcoming Sunday service at High Praise Orlando. It was expected that on this day we could possibly be hearing the decision on the controversial Obergefell v. Hodges case that had been heard by the Supreme Court of the United States of America. This decision from the highest court in the land would determine if issuing same-sex marriage licenses would be made compulsory for all states in our nation. Nine people held this momentous decision in their hands, and we eagerly awaited their decision. As a pastor and a Christian, I hoped and prayed for a righteous pronouncement from the court.

We had prayed for years for a turning of hearts and also prayed against the passing of any legislation that would be in direct rebellion to what God's Word declares on this subject. Jesus made his position clear on this topic: homosexual marriage. Regardless of what we may have heard preached and propagated by some, Jesus did in fact address the issue of homosexuality and same-sex marriage. When Jesus was traveling one day, the Pharisees attempted to trip Him up by asking a question about divorce. Jesus answered in what could be perceived as a somewhat peculiar manner. Let's check out the rebuttal He gave to the question posed by the religious leaders:

> "Have you not read that He who made them at the beginning 'MADE THEM MALE AND FEMALE,' and said, 'For this reason a MAN shall leave his father and mother and be joined to his WIFE, and the two shall become one flesh'? So then, they are no longer two but one flesh. Therefore WHAT GOD HAS JOINED TOGETHER, LET NOT MAN SEPARATE" (Matthew 19:4-6, emphasis added).

To the uninformed, this may appear as if Jesus was almost dismissive regarding the question asked Him by the religious leaders of that day. However, He is not being dismissive in the least. Rather, He went to the foundation of all the universe. He addresses creation, marriage, and the God-ordained union between one man and one woman. Jesus told both the Pharisees and all mankind this simple and timeless truth: GOD DID IT RIGHT! God created a male to marry a female and a female to marry a male. There is simply no other acceptable combination.

Jesus made His point abundantly clear when He said that no man should "separate" themselves from this pattern. Jesus was not simply talking about an individual marriage, but also this pattern of marriage: one man and one woman for one lifetime. Jesus was the final authority on this issue. Individuals can debate and express their futile opinions. However, as

Christians, our position on this issue was settled at creation and reinforced by Jesus. There is no room for an "evolutionary journey" regarding the acceptance of what God calls unacceptable, sin, and an abomination.

Hate Speech or Truth

Contrary to what some have propagated, this is not "hate speech." It is simply the truth of the gospel. We should certainly love all people. Moreover, we should love all of those who are living a sinful lifestyle. Regardless of what the expression of sin may be, we should continue to love people. Furthermore, there is never an excuse to engage in violent behavior directed toward those living in sin. This will certainly not win them to Jesus.

Jesus commanded us to love our neighbors as ourselves (Mark 12:31). The word "neighbor" is not merely referring to people with whom we agree. The Greek word we translate as "neighbor" is *plēsion*. Larry Pierce, creator of the Online Bible, says that word *plēsion* is used as, *according to Christ, any other man irrespective of nation or religion with whom we live or whom we chance to meet.* Realize this love doesn't promote the tolerance of ungodly behavior. Love tells the truth. We can love and still refuse to compromise on the truth of what Jesus has spoken.

I still believe it is possible to both love the sinner and hate the sin in which they are engaging. Jesus certainly loved all people, while still being holy and having no part of sin. If someone is a thief, we should love them. If an individual is a liar, we should love them. Likewise, if someone is involved in a same-sex relationship, we should love them.

With all of that said, we cannot accept sin as a continuing aspect of the life of a born-again believer, and neither should we approve when sin is celebrated and promoted by our culture and government. The moment we adapt the position of moral relativity and compromise in what God's Word says, we lose our position of being salt and light in the earth. When we compromise, we are no longer living a revolutionary lifestyle.

To continue with my story, on that hot and muggy Florida day in June of 2015, I was in the parking lot of a retail store unloading my daughter from her car seat. Suddenly, I received a breaking news alert on my phone. The Supreme Court had ruled five to four in favor of Obergefell. Supreme Court Justices Anthony Kennedy (appointed by President Reagan), Sonia Sotomayor (appointed by President Obama), Ruth Bader Ginsburg (appointed by President Clinton), Elena Kagan (appointed by President Obama), and Stephen Breyer (appointed by President Clinton) were the majority side of the decision ruling to legalize homosexual marriage throughout the United States. This monumental ruling effectively enacted a legal recognition and celebration of ungodliness in our nation. The dichotomy of response was no surprise. Certain segments of society erupted in celebration as they felt they had triumphed. On the other side, many were enraged at this decision from both a moral and state's constitutional rights viewpoint.

I still remember the rollercoaster of emotions that I experienced as I walked holding the hand of my little three-year-old girl. I was initially outraged that this decision was even a possibility in our nation. This nation, according the Mayflower Compact (the first legal document of what would become America), was first settled "for the glory of God, and advancement of the Christian faith." How far had we fallen from that?

As we walked toward the store, I gazed down at my sweet and innocent daughter, and my wrath turned to sadness. Is this the world in which my daughter will be raised? I began to ponder what this meant for us as Christians and furthermore for pastors and other Christian leaders in our nation. My sadness turned to fear. What would those of us who held to a biblical definition of marriage be called? Could there be legal ramifications if we spoke out against this decision and the accompanying lifestyle that was affirmed by it? Ultimately, I felt I was riding in the front row on an emotional rollercoaster that would spin me upside down and drop me for the rest of the day. Space Mountain could not compare to the emotional rollercoaster I was riding.

Looking for some form of encouragement, I decided to check social media to see what leading Christian voices had to say. I checked and saw two major responses from the Church. The first was complete and total silence. Many major leaders had nothing to say at all. The silence was deafening. The second was a response that sounded defeated, deflated, and dejected. To be incredibly transparent, I was falling more into the camp of the second response.

We had prayed, warred, and believed, and this was the final word from the Supreme Court. I felt as if I was in mourning. I was figuratively preparing to wear my sackcloth and smear my forehead with ashes. This proclamation from our government certainly felt like a tipping point. It felt as if we had lost the so-called "culture war."

At a certain point during the day, I realized I needed to plan of how to address this with my congregation. After vacillating throughout the day, I decided I was not going to address this in our church service. I was going to preach an uplifting and encouraging message and just ignore all of this. After all, our congregation doesn't want to be reminded of a setback. They want to hear an encouraging word. At least, that's what I was telling myself. The reality is I wanted to simply bury my head in the sand and act as if nothing had happened. This was not the correct response or attitude needed at that moment.

Just when I had decided my course of action, the Holy Spirit spoke to me and said this, "You weren't made to live in a cave; you were made to prophesy." I immediately felt convicted and broken because of responding in such an immature manner. With all the victories and breakthrough I had experienced, how could one event, one setback, one decision, shake me to my core so radically? Then I remembered there was a great prophet from the Bible who experienced a similar situation and responded in a very similar manner.

Elijah in the Cave

After hearing the voice of the Holy Spirit, my thinking swung toward Elijah and how he had experienced a comparable situation of putting himself in a cave. Let's review this account:

> And Ahab told Jezebel all that Elijah had done, also how he had executed all the prophets with the sword. Then Jezebel sent a messenger to Elijah, saying, "So let the gods do to me, and more also, if I do not make your life as the life of one of them by tomorrow about this time." And when he saw that,

he arose and ran for his life, and went to Beersheba, which belongs to Judah, and left his servant there.

But he himself went a day's journey into the wilderness, and came and sat down under a broom tree. And he prayed that he might die, and said, "It is enough! Now, Lord, take my life, for I am no better than my fathers!"

Then as he lay and slept under a broom tree, suddenly an angel touched him, and said to him, "Arise and eat." Then he looked, and there by his head was a cake baked on coals, and a jar of water. So he ate and drank, and lay down again. And the angel of the Lord came back the second time, and touched him, and said, "Arise and eat, because the journey is too great for you." So he arose, and ate and drank; and he went in the strength of that food forty days and forty nights as far as Horeb, the mountain of God.

And there he went into a cave, and spent the night in that place; and behold, the word of the Lord came to him, and He said to him, "What are you doing here, Elijah?"

So he said, "I have been very zealous for the Lord God of hosts; for the children of Israel have forsaken Your covenant, torn down Your altars, and killed Your prophets with the sword. I alone am left; and they seek to take my life."

Then He said, "Go out, and stand on the mountain before the Lord." And behold, the Lord passed by,

> and a great and strong wind tore into the mountains and broke the rocks in pieces before the Lord, but the Lord was not in the wind; and after the wind an earthquake, but the Lord was not in the earthquake; and after the earthquake a fire, but the Lord was not in the fire; and after the fire a still small voice.
>
> So it was, when Elijah heard it, that he wrapped his face in his mantle and went out and stood in the entrance of the cave. Suddenly a voice came to him, and said, "What are you doing here, Elijah?"
>
> And he said, "I have been very zealous for the Lord God of hosts; because the children of Israel have forsaken Your covenant, torn down Your altars, and killed Your prophets with the sword. I alone am left; and they seek to take my life" (1 Kings 19:1-14).

To fully understand and grasp this passage of Scripture, we must look at the context of what came right before the decree of Jezebel that compelled Elijah to hide in the cave. You would think that it was some sort of tragic setback for Elijah. However, nothing could be further from the truth. What had transpired were some of the events we discussed in the preceding chapter of this book.

Ahab called Elijah a "troubler." (1 Kings 18:7) Elijah challenged Ahab to a showdown with the four hundred fifty prophets of Baal and four hundred prophets of Ashera (1 Kings 18:19). This was followed by the Mount Carmel showdown where the false prophets came up empty while Jehovah answered the call of Elijah by sending fire from heaven. The false prophets were then promptly executed (1 Kings 18:20-

40). Moreover, Elijah proclaimed and prophesied an ending to the drought in Israel and then outran the chariots of King Ahab (1 Kings 18:41-46). All of 1 Kings 18 is filled with victory after victory, triumph after triumph, miracle after miracle, and breakthrough after breakthrough for Elijah.

The amount of victory Elijah experienced during that course of events was staggering. He triumphed over eight hundred fifty false prophets, yet one decree from a governing authority instigated Elijah's retreat to a cave. One pronouncement caused Elijah to forget about his exceedingly great victories. One threat made the prophet of God forget that the Lord answered his cry by sending fire. One decree and he forgot about the rain God sent. One declaration and all was undone in the eyes, heart, and mind of Elijah.

We read this and think to ourselves, "Elijah, how could you be so faithless after everything God has done for you?" However, how many of us, at some point in time, have reacted in the same manner as Elijah? I certainly have! I've probably even reacted that way more than once. We witness miracles, signs, and wonders. This causes us to "ride high" spiritually speaking. However, when there is the first sign of adversity, when things don't go exactly the way we had envisioned, we retreat to a spiritual cave hiding in fear and trepidation.

The prophet Elijah went so far as to say, "It is enough! Now, Lord, take my life" (1 Kings 19:4). This doesn't sound like a victorious prophet. This sounds like an immature whining baby. Elijah, have you forgotten about the victory over the false prophets? Oh, man of God, have you forgotten how God has been with you every step of your ministry? It seems like any time we encounter a setback in the kingdom of God, I hear people say, "I wish Jesus would just come and take us home." While I understand the sentiment and the frustration, this is no different than the pleas and cries of Elijah.

Elijah was still called to have an impact. God couldn't take him up in a chariot just yet. The prophet still had destiny to fulfill. Elijah still had a mission to accomplish. We still have a purpose. God can't take us up just yet. The Church still has a purpose. We can't be removed. We have the answer. What is that purpose? What is that answer? Our purpose is the answer. Revolutionaries are called to pour out oil and prophesy.

Oil is the Answer

I am going to make what may seem like a bold statement: **the answer to every problem we face in our world today is found in the people of God coming out of the cave and releasing the anointing of God.** We must stop hiding and start pouring out oil! We can no longer sit on the sidelines and allow Jezebel to rule. We must prophesy. Look at what God says to Elijah in 1 Kings 19 while the prophet is still in the cave.

> Then the Lord said to him: "Go, return on your way to the Wilderness of Damascus; and when you arrive, anoint Hazael as king over Syria. Also you shall anoint Jehu the son of Nimshi as king over Israel. And Elisha the son of Shaphat of Abel Meholah you shall anoint as prophet in your place. It shall be that whoever escapes the sword of Hazael, Jehu will kill; and whoever escapes the sword of Jehu, Elisha will kill. Yet I have reserved seven thousand in Israel, all whose knees have not bowed to Baal, and every mouth that has not kissed

> him." So he departed from there, and found Elisha the son of Shaphat (1 Kings 19:15-19).

Israel was plagued by the tyrannical rule of Ahab and Jezebel that had allowed idolatry and immorality to reign. Those evil monarchs had attempted to silence God's people and had brought Israel to the worship of false and pagan gods. Anyone who didn't give Jezebel exactly what she wanted was executed. Remember Naboth and his vineyard (1 Kings 21:1-16).

Something must be done about dictatorial rulers. However, nothing can be accomplished when the one who has the answer—the one who has been anointed—is hiding in a cave. God told Elijah: get out of the cave and begin to release an anointing; begin to pour out oil. The Lord told Elijah to anoint Hazael as King of Persia, Jehu as King of Israel, and Elisha as the future prophet to replace him (1 Kings 19:15-18). The process of anointing involved these men being marked and having oil poured or smeared on them.

Everything that was needed to see the abolishment of the tyrannical regime was inside of Elijah. However, the prophet needed to leave the cave and prophesy and release an anointing! Nothing has changed. God's answer to apostasy in society is still the same; prophets must leave the cave and release an anointing.

Jezebel and Ahab: Alive and Well

Let me say this, the spirit of Jezebel and Ahab is still very much alive today. As a matter of fact, all the immorality that we are facing today, somewhere in the mix is the spirit of Ahab and Jezebel. Jesus warns the church at Thyatira, the corrupt church, about their passive stance toward Jezebel. This was spoken to that church nearly a millennium after Jezebel's time on earth had ended. The spirit of Jezebel promotes perversion and everything against godly standards. At Thyatira, this manifested in sexual immorality and compromise running rampant in the gathering of believers (Revelation 2:18-23). The spirit of Ahab, while not necessarily complicit with the activity of Jezebel, stands idle and silently refuses to confront what Jezebel is engaging.

While the spirit of Jezebel reigns in our land, the spirit of Ahab fills many pulpits with people afraid to say anything—afraid to speak out and afraid to take a stand. What is the solution to this problem? Revolutionaries with the spirit of Elijah must arise.

The Breaker Anointing

While Ahab and Jezebel reign, many in our society live bound by principalities and powers. Remember, it is the anointing that breaks the yoke of bondage (Isaiah 10:27). It's time we come out of the cave and begin to smear the oil of God on those whom He has called. Whether we are in full-time ministry, work a secular job, are a homemaker, or are retired, we are called to release an anointing in this day and hour. The breaker anointing is released when we pour out oil.

Amid the rumblings, threatening, and ungodly decrees of society, it is the still the anointing that is victorious. However, to see Jezebel thrown down, we must get on the offensive. We must arise and leave the cave. It is time to quit hiding and start fighting!

Get Offensive

Being in the cave was living in a defensive posture. God didn't call His Church to live defensively, but rather offensively. We aren't called to be hunted; we are called to be the hunters. Somewhere in our history we have taken a twisted perspective of believing that because we are called to be meek, that somehow equals being weak. Nothing could be further from the truth. Meekness and weakness are not the same. The Church is called to be powerful and to preemptively strike the enemy. I don't wait for the enemy to attack me to fight back; I hit first. Some may think this sounds extreme. However, this type of thinking was propagated and supported by Jesus. Look at what He said to His disciples, specifically Simon Peter:

> When Jesus came into the region of Caesarea Philippi, He asked His disciples, saying, "Who do men say that I, the Son of Man, am?" So they said, "Some say John the Baptist, some Elijah, and others Jeremiah or one of the prophets." He said to them, "But who do you say that I am?" Simon Peter answered and said, "You are the Christ, the Son of the living God." Jesus answered and said to him, "Blessed are you, Simon Bar-Jonah, for flesh and blood has not revealed this to you, but My Father who is in heaven. And I also say to you that you are Peter, and on this rock I will build My church, and the gates of Hades shall not prevail against it (Matthew 16:13-18).

As someone who was raised in church my entire life and now in my thirties, I can't tell you how many times I have heard the verse found in Matthew 16:18 quoted. Every time I heard this passage, I envisioned a defensive stand. Let me explain. My interpretation was that we would be tested, but we will hang on until the end and persevere. The kingdoms of hell were going to attack us, but we would be able to fend off the attack, but just barely. Let me tell you, that is not the picture Jesus is painting at all. As a matter of fact, His words paint a portrait of a principle that is the exact opposite.

Storm the Gates

I love movies and books set in the medieval era. I am especially fond of fantasy movies and books like ***Lord of the Rings*** and ***The Chronicles of Narnia*** which have a fantastical medieval vibe to them. Some of my favorite parts pertaining to the genre are the battle scenes. Often, these clashes involve someone defending a castle against an invading force. If the aggressors are ever able to breech the gates of the castle, they will overrun the defenders and be victorious. If they successfully storm the gates, they get the victory. I know this may seem obvious, but realize that GATES are NOT OFFENSIVE; they are DEFENSIVE. You are not able to inflict damage with a gate. Rather, gates attempt to repel damage.

Jesus said the gates of hell would not prevail against the Church. We have twisted it to be the other way. Understand, Jesus never intended for His Church to have a defensive stand. We are intended to storm the gates of hell. However, we can't be offensive when we back down at the threatening of hell. All the enemy has is empty threats. Remember, as we said in an earlier chapter, the enemy is like a roaring lion with no teeth. The prince of the power of the air understands that when we leave the cave and storm the gates, his time is limited.

Revolutionaries are those who lead the charge against the gates of hell. According to the words of Jesus, when we make the choice to storm the gates, hell will not prevail. If hell will not prevail, that means that we, the Church, will win. In my mind's eye, I can see forces of revolutionaries awakened to this kingdom reality. This amassed force is storming the gates and being victorious. We must leave the cave and begin to lead the charge to see victory realized. Revolutionaries, assemble and storm the gates!

Just One Generation Away

Elijah wisely chose to heed the voice of the Lord and leave the cave. Upon leaving the damp and dark cave, Elijah found Elisha and threw his mantle on him. Then Elisha made the choice to follow Elijah as he embraced the mantle of sonship. Ultimately, Elisha anointed both Jehu as King of Judah and Hazael as King of Syria.

Once Elijah left the cave he rediscovered boldness. The prophet was no longer cowering. Elijah, at the prompting of God, began to prophesy the death of Jezebel. The one who had threatened to kill the prophet is now the subject of Elijah's prophetic proclamation of death. The hunted has now become the hunter. The prophet was now decreeing her ultimate end. Not only was Elijah prophesying the end of Jezebel, but also of the entire lineage of Ahab and Jezebel. Imagine the boldness, Elijah prophesied it to the face of King Ahab. Wow! Check out the strong and bold prophetic decree of this man of God:

> Then the word of the Lord came to Elijah the Tishbite, saying, "Arise, go down to meet Ahab king of Israel, who lives in Samaria. There he is, in the

> vineyard of Naboth, where he has gone down to take possession of it. You shall speak to him, saying, 'Thus says the Lord: "Have you murdered and also taken possession?"' And you shall speak to him, saying, 'Thus says the Lord: "In the place where dogs licked the blood of Naboth, dogs shall lick your blood, even yours."'" So Ahab said to Elijah, "Have you found me, O my enemy?" And he answered, "I have found you, because you have sold yourself to do evil in the sight of the Lord: 'Behold, I will bring calamity on you. I will take away your posterity, and will cut off from Ahab every male in Israel, both bond and free. I will make your house like the house of Jeroboam the son of Nebat, and like the house of Baasha the son of Ahijah, because of the provocation with which you have provoked Me to anger, and made Israel sin.' And concerning Jezebel the Lord also spoke, saying, 'The dogs shall eat Jezebel by the wall of Jezreel.' The dogs shall eat whoever belongs to Ahab and dies in the city, and the birds of the air shall eat whoever dies in the field" (1 Kings 21:17-24).

Elijah was a new man with a new fire. Any fear, trepidation, and timidity had been left in the cave. When we make the choice to leave the cave, we find a new confidence in our anointing. Elijah anointed Elisha and prophesied Jezebel's undoing. This is still the blueprint for victory in the earth today: anoint God's people and prophesy the end of the enemy.

If we look forward to 2 Kings chapter 9, Elijah had been taken up in the chariot and Ahab had died. Jezebel still reigned as Queen Regent while her son Jehoram was king of the Northern

Kingdom of Israel. Furthermore, Jezebel's grandson, Ahaziah, was King of Judah. The seed of Ahab and Jezebel still reigned in the earth. If anything, they had gained power since the prophetic decree of Elijah. However, all that changed in one day. Why? If we trace it back, it is due to the fact that Elijah didn't stay in the cave. Jezebel was soon to meet her end because Elijah prophesied what God would do in the earth.

Elisha, acting as the prophet, sent a servant to anoint Jehu as God had directed Elijah to do when he left the cave (2 Kings 9:1-11). Some have wondered why Elijah wasn't the one to physically anoint Jehu. While I don't have the total answer, it could be simply because he never encountered Jehu to anoint him. It was obviously not yet the season for fulfillment. Moreover, Elisha as a spiritual son, completed the work that God began in Elijah.

Ultimately, the day came and Jehu was anointed king. Immediately, a group of warriors rallied around him and proclaimed him as rightful ruler. These mighty men rode out to face King Jehoram and King Ahaziah (2 Kings 9:12-14). Look at what happened when an anointed warrior stepped up to fulfill prophecy declared by the prophet Elijah.

> So Jehu rode in a chariot and went to Jezreel, for Joram was laid up there; and Ahaziah king of Judah had come down to see Joram. Now a watchman stood on the tower in Jezreel, and he saw the company of Jehu as he came, and said, "I see a company of men." And Joram said, "Get a horseman and send him to meet them, and let him say, 'Is it peace?'" So the horseman went to meet him, and said, "Thus says the king: 'Is it peace?'" And Jehu

said, "What have you to do with peace? Turn around and follow me." So the watchman reported, saying, "The messenger went to them, but is not coming back." Then he sent out a second horseman who came to them, and said, "Thus says the king: 'Is it peace?'" And Jehu answered, "What have you to do with peace? Turn around and follow me." So the watchman reported, saying, "He went up to them and is not coming back; and the driving is like the driving of Jehu the son of Nimshi, for he drives furiously!"

Then Joram said, "Make ready." And his chariot was made ready. Then Joram king of Israel and Ahaziah king of Judah went out, each in his chariot; and they went out to meet Jehu, and met him on the property of Naboth the Jezreelite. Now it happened, when Joram saw Jehu, that he said, "Is it peace, Jehu?" So he answered, "What peace, as long as the harlotries of your mother Jezebel and her witchcraft are so many?"

Then Joram turned around and fled, and said to Ahaziah, "Treachery, Ahaziah!" Now Jehu drew his bow with full strength and shot Jehoram between his arms; and the arrow came out at his heart, and he sank down in his chariot. Then Jehu said to Bidkar his captain, "Pick him up, and throw him into the tract of the field of Naboth the Jezreelite; for remember, when you and I were riding together behind Ahab his father, that the Lord laid this burden upon him: 'Surely I saw yesterday the blood of Naboth and the blood of his sons,' says the Lord,

> 'and I will repay you in this plot,' says the Lord. Now therefore, take and throw him on the plot of ground, according to the word of the Lord." But when Ahaziah king of Judah saw this, he fled by the road to Beth Haggan. So Jehu pursued him, and said, "Shoot him also in the chariot." And they shot him at the Ascent of Gur, which is by Ibleam. Then he fled to Megiddo, and died there (2 Kings 9:16-27).

Wow! In one moment, in one day, the reigning seed of Ahab and Jezebel were struck down from their place of ruling over God's people. No longer would they promote and propagate ungodliness, uncleanness, and unrighteousness in Israel. Furthermore, Jehu rode to Jezreel and saw to it that once and for all, Jezebel, the one who had threatened the man of God, met her end. Jehu watched as two or three eunuchs, victims of the treachery of Jezebel, threw her down from her window and she died. (2 Kings 9:30-37) The word of the Lord released through Elijah after his leaving the cave was fulfilled. Moreover, Ahab's seventy sons, his closest acquaintances, all who remained in his house, all of his priests, Ahaziah's forty-two brothers, the rest of Ahab's family, and all the remaining prophets of Baal were all put to death. The evil of Jezebel, Ahab, and Baal worship had been wiped out of Israel completely (2 Kings 10:1-29).

None of this could have happened unless a prophet released a word. He couldn't release the word of the Lord while cowering in a cave. The prophetic word was designed to be announced and proclaimed loudly and unashamedly, not whispered in hiding. Because of Elijah's faithfulness, in one generation the stain of the rule of Ahab and Jezebel was obliterated and washed away. Not only that, there was no longer a chance for their seed to pervert Israel again.

We do not wrestle with flesh and blood. However, there is a spiritual war with real and tangible stakes. There are actual principalities and powers that are causing ungodliness and unrighteousness to rule in our world just as it did in the days of Elijah. A dear friend of mine, Pastor Judy Jacobs, famously sings a song entitled "Days of Elijah." I really do believe we are living in the days of Elijah. As in his time, we must arise and begin to declare the word of the Lord in the earth. We must not cower and hide in this hour. As we begin to release an anointing and prophesy, as we act with the spirit of the revolutionary, the tide is turning in our day.

I believe we can see a turning in one generation. It took many generations of complacency for us to arrive in the current situation we find ourselves. However, I believe if we leave the cave, just as Elijah did, we can see the same results Elijah experienced. In one generation, we can see victory realized. Revolutionary, do not fear. Rather, put your trust in God, fulfill your purpose, leave the cave, anoint God's people, and prophesy the end to what has brought idolatry and ungodliness to our shores. It is time to come out of the cave and prophesy. O Revolutionary, release the word God has placed within you!

CHAPTER 9

GLORY IN THE VALLEY

In the second chapter of this book, we talked in detail about the Battle of Yorktown; the battle that essentially concluded the American War for Independence. Following the signing of the articles of capitulation, people marched in the streets and celebrated the victory of the American revolutionaries. Following years of bloodshed, starvation, losses, and despair, the vision these men had of a free nation was realized. This must have been an incredible mountaintop experience for them.

The elation experienced by men like George Washington, Alexander Hamilton, Marquis de Lafayette, and Comte de Rochambeau who fought at Yorktown must have been palpable. Furthermore, as the news of the victory at Yorktown spread to Thomas Jefferson, John Adams, and Benjamin Franklin, the emotions were surely running high. Despite overwhelming odds, they were free, independent, and most of all, victorious. However, they didn't merely set out to win a war, but rather to see freedom brought to the inhabitants of the original thirteen colonies. They didn't fight because they wanted to engage in battle. The struggle was about seeing freedom brought to the oppressed inhabitants of the colonies. Their warfare was for a purpose.

The purpose of being a spiritual revolutionary isn't to simply fight for the sake of fighting. We aren't troublers because we are simply those who want to cause a problem and be a proverbial pain in the neck. We don't prophesy because we like to hear our voices echo. We have a vision and a purpose.

Just as the revolutionaries of colonial America, we engage in great struggle to release freedom to the captives. In colonial America, what was in the hearts and minds of these brilliant men were brought into a place of reality. Freedom had come to the colonies.

Mountaintop Experiences

The life of the spiritual revolutionary may be filled with setback, opposition, and at times even disappointment. The American revolutionaries went through all of this. However, that is all outweighed by moments of elation, fulfillment, and glory. I call these moments "mountaintop experiences." Every victory realized over the enemy is a mountaintop experience. Every encounter with the tangible presence of Holy Spirit is a mountaintop experience. While these experiences of victory are incredible, they are not the objective of being a revolutionary. These experiences are not the end-game. As a revolutionary, we will have victory in spiritual battle against principalities and powers. However, this mountaintop experience is not the ultimate end of our purpose.

The purpose of the mountaintop is to propel us to release glory in the valley. This is the model that Jesus showed his closest disciples: Peter, James, and John. Look at this account with me.

> Now after six days Jesus took Peter, James, and John his brother, led them up on a high mountain by themselves; and He was transfigured before them. His face shone like the sun, and His clothes became as white as the light. And behold, Moses and Elijah appeared to them, talking with Him. Then Peter answered and said to Jesus, "Lord, it is good for us to be here; if You wish, let us make here three tabernacles: one for You, one for Moses, and one for Elijah." While he was still speaking, behold, a bright cloud overshadowed them; and suddenly a voice came out of the cloud, saying, "This is My beloved Son, in whom I am well pleased. Hear Him!" And when the disciples heard it, they fell on their faces and were greatly afraid. But Jesus came and touched them and said, "Arise, and do not be afraid." When they had lifted up their eyes, they saw no one but Jesus only. Now as they came down from the mountain, Jesus commanded them, saying, "Tell the vision to no one until the Son of Man is risen from the dead" (Matthew 17:1-9).

What an incredible passage and experience for these men. I don't know if there is a more magnificent account in Scripture. Jesus was revealed in the fullness of His glory on that mountain. Wow! His face shone as bright as the sun.

I can recall being a child riding in my parent's car. I occasionally attempted to look at the sun for as long as I could. My gaze could not stay focused on the sun for long due to the intensity of light radiating which caused my eyes to hurt. That was the brilliance with which the face of Jesus shone on that day. His face must have been difficult to behold due to the brilliant light that shone forth.

Jesus appeared with Elijah on one side and Moses on the other. Whoa, I get overwhelmed with emotion just thinking about this. The manifestation of the Law and the Prophets stood with Jesus. Two of the greatest giants in all of Scripture stood with the incarnate Son of God. Furthermore, the voice of Father God audibly came from heaven and once again announced His pleasure in Jesus. This was the glory of God manifest. This was undoubtedly the most glorious encounter any man had ever participated in recorded history.

Peter, James, and John were totally, utterly, and completely blown away. The three closest disciples of Jesus were enamored. Two of the three were speechless. Peter saw Jesus in His intrinsic and incarnate glory. The one whom Jesus would later say possessed the rock upon which the Church would be built (Matthew 16:18) has a literal mountaintop experience.

How did Peter react? The same way that we do today. Peter wanted to stay on the mountain. Because of Peter's experience, he proclaimed, "Let's just stay right here." Peter even says, "It is good for us to be here" (Matthew 17:4). The problem was that it wasn't good for those in the valley to stay in that position. He continued, we can build a tabernacle for You (Jesus), a tabernacle for Moses, and a tabernacle for Elijah. We can devise a method to shuttle everyone up here and let them experience this glory. Jesus does not concur with Peter on his suggestion. Jesus doesn't say, "Good idea Peter, let's get to building those temples."

What is interesting is that Jesus didn't even acknowledge what Simon Peter said. As a matter of fact, the Father interrupted Peter with a voice echoing from the heavenlies and didn't even allow him to finish his thought process. What Peter didn't realize is that the glory was not displayed on the mountaintop so they could stay there and begin a building project. The mountaintop was to propel them to the valley. **The glory in the mountain was intended to be displayed in the valley.** Jesus simply touched his three closest followers, started back down the mountain, and went to the valley.

Go to the Valley

As great as the glory is on the mountaintop, you and I weren't made for that moment. Revolutionaries are called to the valley. I have been part of some incredible and glorious services and encounters with God. There isn't a service that goes by at High Praise where we don't sense the tangible presence of Holy Spirit in some manner. Even during Wednesday night Bible study, the presence of Holy Spirit is always profound. Even though it is a common occurrence, it never ceases to amaze me when we encounter His glory.

I was recently in a service where a prophetic utterance came forth and it sent chills down my spine due to the accuracy of the word released. A prodigal son was called out by name and pronouncement was made that he would be in service the next day to surrender his life back to God. The next day, I witnessed the fulfillment of the word. That man was in the service and indeed surrendered his life back to God while having no knowledge of the word prophesied the previous day. The mountaintop is amazing and filled with inconceivable manifestation and satisfaction.

I can recall so many church services where I did not even want to leave the building where we met. There were many times where our worship team continued to play on after service was dismissed. We were doing more than just "jamming" as musicians. There was a tangible glory and presence of God. We were on top of the mountain and didn't want to leave.

Though these are wonderful and glorious moments, that is not where a revolutionary fulfills destiny. I've been like Peter and said, "Jesus, can we just stay in this place? Can we just stay in this glory forever?" The Lord, much like He did with Peter, simply has tapped me and said, "Let's go. There are hurting and oppressed people in the valley. Go release freedom."

There are so many believers that want to live basking in His glory at the top of the mountain being separated from the activity of the world. However, their ultimate purpose isn't at the top of the mountain. Jesus called them to go the valley. He shows us the purpose for the mountaintop as He comes down from the Mount of Transfiguration. The mountaintop experience, encouragement, and elation are to propel us to the multitudes of hurting and broken people living in the low place. Let's look at Jesus in the valley:

> And when they had come to the multitude, a man came to Him, kneeling down to Him and saying, "Lord, have mercy on my son, for he is an epileptic and suffers severely; for he often falls into the fire and often into the water. So I brought him to Your disciples, but they could not cure him." Then Jesus answered and said, "O faithless and perverse generation, how long shall I be with you? How long shall I bear with you? Bring him here to Me." And Jesus rebuked the demon, and it came out of him; and the child was cured from that very hour (Matthew 17:14-18).

Firstly, we see the contrast between the mountaintop and the valley. At the top of the mountain, in the glory, there was Jesus, Peter, James, and John (not counting the appearances of Elijah and Moses). Meanwhile, in the valley there is a multitude. The people in the valley outnumber the people who have experienced His glory in a real and tangible way.

Look at society today and we see this scenario mirrored. Even many people who call themselves Christians have infrequently (if ever) had a real encounter with God's power. No matter how big of a conference you have been to where you experienced an outpouring of His presence, there are over seven billion people on earth. There are more in the valley that haven't experienced His glory and power than those who have tasted it. However, they need to experience His power in a real way.

Understand, the people still dwelling in the valley have issues for which the only answer is the anointing. The people in the valley are still living in the chains and oppression of the enemy. The only answer to their problem is an encounter with Jesus. Earlier we made this proclamation: the anointing is the answer to every issue we have in society. Jesus demonstrated that the encounter on the mountaintop should compel us to release the anointing in the valley.

Dysfunction in the Valley

In the valley, Jesus was approached by a man who had a son tormented with epilepsy. He was bound by this disorder and dysfunction. The valley is full of dysfunction and disorder. The disorder placed the life of this young man in severe danger as he often fell in fire and water. The young man's father brought him to the disciples of Jesus, but there had been no fruit of change.

Judging from the context of the account, I believe that the nine disciples who had not been on the mountain attempted to bring freedom to this young man, but to no avail. Why? Could it be that they had yet to experience His glory manifested like it was on the mountaintop? I believe so. You cannot release glory unless you have first experienced His glory.

It would not be until they had an encounter with the glory and power of God in the "upper room" (a type of the mountaintop) that they moved in miracles, signs, and wonders. The disciples had been commissioned by Jesus, but without experiencing glory they had no authority to release miracles and freedom to the captives. The problem was not an unwillingness on their part to obey the assignment they had been given. They simply had yet to receive the power that could only be released through the mountaintop experience.

So, this desperate father had a son who was living in dysfunction until he had an encounter with a Man who had come from the mountaintop. Moreover, when glory shows up in the valley everything changed for this young man and his father. Healing was released and nothing was ever the same for them.

More Than a Cool Show

Jesus didn't take Peter, James, and John up the mountain simply because He wanted to have a mountain climbing expedition, put on a cool special effects show, and have a meet-and-greet with Elijah and Moses. Jesus revealed the glory and subsequently releases His power to the broken. You see, He knew that CHRIST, THE HOPE OF GLORY would abide in them. (Colossians 1:27) He knew they were going to receive the Holy Ghost and the *dunamis*, miracle working power! Jesus demonstrated the manifestation of glory that would live inside of them and what that glory was intended to produce. Jesus exemplified that they needed to release heaven on earth in the valley. Revolutionaries possess this same power (*dunamis*) and authority (*exousia*). This is the purpose of our calling.

We don't lay hands on the sick, preach the gospel, prophesy, and cast out demons because we want to put on a "cool show." It's more than giving a "good talk" when we minister. Our mission is to see lives transformed by the supernatural power of God.

I had someone recently ask me, "What is on the other side of revolution?" The answer to me is really simple. It is the governing authority and culture of heaven manifested tangibly in the earth. In heaven, there is no sickness, disease, poverty, oppression, depression, or demonic principalities. It's not for another day or season; it is right now.

Heaven on Earth

When Jesus healed this young man, the Son of David was enforcing heaven on earth. What was the inheritance of man due to the fall? Our inheritance was sickness. However, sickness is defeated because Jesus came to pay the price so heaven could be released here and now! Jesus came to bring a new order, a new government, and a new kingdom. The kingdom of heaven: here and now. That is exactly what Jesus taught his disciples when he taught them to pray.

> Now it came to pass, as He was praying in a certain place, when He ceased, that one of His disciples said to Him, "Lord, teach us to pray, as John also taught his disciples." So He said to them, "When you pray, say: Our Father in heaven, Hallowed be Your name. Your kingdom come. Your will be done On earth as it is in heaven (Luke 11:1-2).

After extolling and glorifying the Father, the next thing Jesus instructed them to pray is for His Kingdom to come. The word "kingdom" is from the Greek word *basileia* which means *rule of a realm*. Jesus said they are to pray that the Kingdom of the Father will reign in the realm of earth.

There are so many Christians who are looking to escape this realm and go to heaven. However, Jesus said pray the kingdom of heaven into this realm. Pray that the Father will rule in this realm. God already reigns over all the universe. However, Jesus commands us to pray that His reign be made evident in the earth.

How can we tell when someone is in charge and reigning over a realm? It is simple. It is when their laws and culture are enforced. In the culture of the kingdom of heaven, epilepsy does not exist. When Jesus healed this young man, the Savior put into action with His prayer, the kingdom of God manifested.

The Government of God

There are many believers who have relinquished authority in the earth to the enemy by default. Why? It is because they have bought into the idea that this world doesn't belong to God, but rather the enemy. Thus, we have abandoned our proper place of governing authority. This world does not belong to satan and his minions. Nothing could be further from the truth. The psalmist said, "The earth is the Lord's, and all its fullness" (Psalm 24:1). If this truth was relevant in the Old Testament, it is all the more true today.

Furthermore, even before Jesus was born into earth, prophets decreed what would happen through his ministry and life. Look at what the prophet Isaiah said.

> For unto us a Child is born, Unto us a Son is given; And the government will be upon His shoulder. And His name will be called Wonderful, Counselor, Mighty God, Everlasting Father, Prince of Peace. Of the increase of His government and peace there will be no end (Isaiah 9:6-7).

Government is mentioned twice in these two verses. The government being upon the shoulders of Jesus is the first thing that the prophet Isaiah indicates. The word "government" is from the Hebrew word *misrah* which means *empire*. Isaiah did not merely say Jesus is going to carry the government. No, he declared that the empire of Jesus was going to increase. The empire of the kingdom of God is meant to increase until the second-coming of Christ. However, Jesus had to come to make this possible.

Forfeited Authority

When God created man, He gave Adam dominion in the earth (Genesis 1:26). The word "dominion" is from the Hebrew word *radah*; it means *to tread down, subjugate, rule, and reign.*

God gave man authority to rule and reign in the earth. God gave man such authority that he could actually surrender his dominion to another party. That is exactly what happened when Adam and Eve disobeyed God and fell. They forfeited their authority to the enemy and began to live under the curse.

For the next four thousand years, mankind lived under the dominion of the serpent. The people watching for the Messiah heard prophetic utterances and yearned for the day that man had relationship and covenant with God once again. However, they lived under the dominion of the enemy, until...! I love that last word. It's until Jesus came to put the government of earth back on His shoulders as Isaiah prophesied.

Jesus began His ministry at thirty-years-old and ministered to the multitudes throughout Israel for three years. In the end, Jesus went to a place called Mount Calvary, the ultimate mountaintop experience. The greatest act of intercession in history happened on that day when the kingdom of hell was broken and the kingdom of God restored. Through the shedding of the blood of Jesus, the rule and reign of Almighty God was reinstated in the earth. Dominion returned to people of covenant once again!

Because of His redemptive and restorative act on the cross, we once again have a covenant and relationship with God. This new covenant also restores to us the authority that was lost in the fall. The enemy is not in charge of the world. We have been made ambassadors of the kingdom of heaven to enforce His kingdom in the earth here and now. We are no longer crying for the days of the kingdom of God to come, we are living to enforce the kingdom of God.

There Comes a Day

Let's go back to the days of the American Revolution once again. Men like George Washington, John Adams, Thomas Jefferson, and Alexander Hamilton had a vision for what they believed America was called to be. These men were not perfect, but they were men with a vision. For this reason, they fought and waged war. They fought to see a government established in the earth. However, after Yorktown there came a point in time where they were no longer fighting to see the right to rule as they had envisioned. The time of governing had come.

They wrote decrees and documents explaining this new government. These brilliant men met together and worked out a new system of government that we experience in America to this very day. Everyone within the colonies were not happy about this new government or the victory of the colonists. However, because of their victory in warfare, they had earned the right to rule. Those who are victorious in warfare will always be those who rule.

The same is true in the spirit realm. Those who are willing to fight, war, and see victory will rule and reign. The good news is that because of what Jesus accomplished, the fight is fixed and we are victorious in battle!

Remember, during the American Revolution, there existed a group of people who remained loyal to the Crown of England. I know we picture everyone being all on-board for the American War for Independence, but that simply wasn't the case. Historians speculate that the percentage of those in the colonies who remained loyal to King George III amid the revolution ranged from between 15 and 20 percent of the inhabitants of America. Even though these loyalists had pledged allegiance to the Crown, they were suddenly governed by the revolutionaries. Likewise, we cannot become distracted by people who want to remain loyal to the system of the world. We must press forward and release freedom to those living in bondage.

Freedom Has Come

Just as the average American colonist found freedom after a mountaintop experience (Battle of Yorktown), the young epileptic man in the valley found freedom after a mountaintop experience through the ministry of the ultimate revolutionary, Jesus. Spiritual revolutionaries are going to experience some incredible things in God on the mountaintop. However, our life consists of more than just an experience and flying high. We are called to release freedom to those still in the valley.

Yes, we fight for freedom. Yes, we contend for liberty. Yes, we announce and proclaim it. These things happen and are realized on the mountaintop. However, there comes a point where we go to those in bondage and let them know they can now be free just as we are free. It is time for revolutionaries to shift their perspective from living in the mountaintop experience to releasing what is found at the top of the mountain to those living in the valley of despair.

There are billions of people in this world living in the valley. They are wrapped in chains, bondage, and dysfunction. They are awaiting someone to proclaim with a shout of victory, "Freedom is here!" Moreover, they are looking for someone with the sword to destroy their chains of bondage. Remember, John the beloved, who was on the mountain with the Lord, told us that Jesus came to destroy the works of the enemy (1 John 3:8). Could it be that when John wrote this, one of the things he recalled in his memory was the young man who experienced freedom from epilepsy in the valley? I believe so.

We are called to be imitators of the greatest revolutionary, Jesus (1 Corinthians 11:1, Ephesians 5:1, 1 John 2:6). It is time for us to release glory in the valley and break the chains of the enemy that have bound individuals. Revolutionaries desire to see His kingdom come right here and now! Let the kingdom of Jesus reign! Let the revolutionaries be on the forefront announcing His kingdom has come!

CHAPTER 10

OVERCOMING FAITH

> For whatever is born of God overcomes the world. And this is the victory that has overcome the world—our faith. Who is he who overcomes the world, but he who believes that Jesus is the Son of God? (1 John 5:4-5)

I cannot think of a single Scripture more important for the time in which we currently live. We need to read this Scripture repeatedly. We need to make this a daily confession over our lives. It must become our declaration of faith. This is the creed of the revolutionary. What John wrote should be the battle cry of spiritual revolutionaries the world over. We can never forget this simple fact; we are destined to overcome the world. It is the promise of His Word.

Regardless of what your theological perspective may be, if we simply take this Scripture at face value, we have overcome the world. The Greek word that is translated "world" in this verse of Scripture is the word *kosmos*. It means *the world in a wide or narrow sense, including its inhabitants.* Let me put it this way. Regardless of how you look at the world, we as believers are called to overcome it. If we are going to be revolutionaries, we must believe this.

I think that the Founding Fathers who fought in the American Revolution believed and had confidence that they would ultimately overcome. I do not think they would have been willing to literally put their necks on the line had they not had a confident expectation of victory. If we want to define faith into a very basic and simplistic definition it could be defined this way, *a confident unshakeable expectation*. We can have a confident unshakeable expectation of victory over the world because Jesus assured us that we have already won.

Reality Check

Now time for a reality check. When I stand and look at society today, it seems as if the Church and the nations of the earth are swallowed up by a rising tide of immorality. Personally, I can barely stand to turn on the news as we see Christians and biblical values maligned by the majority of media outlets both large and small. It does not matter whether you read a newspaper, watch cable, or search internet sites, the perspective is largely negative toward morality and Christianity. The slant increases as time goes by.

I have begun to understand the philosophy of the great man of God called the Apostle of Faith, Smith Wigglesworth. Wigglesworth refused to allow a newspaper in his home. If we allow our gaze to be more focused on media than His Word, it can negatively affect our faith.

Hollywood has intensified their attempt to villainize Christians and the Church to an even greater level. I recently saw a comedy skit from a very popular television show that was mocking the idea of the genuine and real persecution that Christians endure for taking a stand for their moral and biblical values. Their attempt at comedy fell far short of humor. I was not amused; it's shocking and disheartening.

We see the statistics saying that millennials are less interested in the Church and Christianity than any generation who have come previously. This excites many in the contemporary culture feeling as if "organized religion" is in its dying days. With waning influence from the Church, should the fact that we have never seen a generation more confused about gender identity and sexuality be a surprise?

In our culture today, we have men who think they are women, women who think they are men, and these people are called heroes, and they grace the covers of magazines the world over. We have men who want to sleep with men and women who want to sleep with women. These people are heralded as "trail-blazers" and the "new normal" in society. These things are to say the least ungodly, perverse, and defy the very nature for which God created man and woman. Meanwhile, Christians who take a stand are called intolerant, haters, and even bigots. These things would have been unimaginable just twenty years ago. However, these are realities we are currently facing in the world in which we live.

Even within the walls of the church, there is a rising tide of worldliness. The Church has become more of a reflection of the culture than the called-out ones changing culture. We see more and more pastors and leaders falling into sin and heresy. Therefore, it should be of no surprise to see the same happening in the pews.

Is there anything we can do to stop the onslaught and put a halt to the consistent slide to where our society is headed?

Unfortunately, if you ask some believers or just listen to their manner of conversation, you would think that the answer is "no." However, I am so glad that they are not the ones who have the deciding vote.

Victory in Jesus

Jesus announced a decision. He rendered a verdict two thousand years ago when He was nailed to a cross on a hill called Calvary. The good news is this: Jesus' decision was in our favor. He gave us victory at the cross! He rendered a verdict that said this: WORLD, YOU HAVE BEEN DEFEATED! WORLD, YOU HAVE BEEN OVERCOME! CHURCH, YOU ARE VICTORIOUS! Praise God for victory realized through the precious blood of Jesus.

John reinforced the concept of victory over the world in the passage quoted at the beginning of this chapter (1 John 5:4-5). Moreover, the apostle told us what causes us to see the victory enforced; he tells us that it is our faith that overcomes the world. If we want to live the life of a spiritual revolutionary, we must live with what I call *overcoming faith*! We are not called to be vanquished; we are called to be victorious. The Church is not called to be conquered; we are called to be conquerors. We must change our perspective. We must have the perspective of overcoming faith.

What is Overcoming Faith?

The word "overcome" that John uses in this epistle is from the Greek word *nikaō*. It means *to conquer, prevail, and get the victory*. The word for "faith" is translated from the Greek word *pistis* and its definition is as follows: *persuasion, credence, or moral conviction*. So, overcoming faith is a moral conviction that we have the victory. Overcoming faith is a persuasion that we have conquered. Overcoming faith is credence to the fact that we have prevailed.

People with the perspective of overcoming faith are those who are persuaded that the only acceptable outcome is victory. It doesn't matter what they may see at a given time; they walk by faith and not by sight. They live by what they believe, rather than what they see. Revolutionaries believe that victory belongs to them. Regardless of what things may look like in our culture right now, I have overcoming faith. Our faith **WILL** overcome the world.

Many who have already conceded defeat in our culture today lack faith to believe for victory. I totally understand the temptation to just say, "Forget it," and then go hide in the cave similarly to the prophet Elijah. However, when we have a perspective of overcoming faith, we refuse to quit until the desired outcome is seen. God's desired outcome is found in 1 John 5 where it declares, "Whatever is born of God overcomes the world." Regardless of what we may see, we are overcomers.

Not by Sight

In 2 Corinthians 5:7, Paul said this, "For we walk by faith, not by sight." If there was ever an age in which it is important for us to cling to this spiritual reality, it is now. We need to understand that our sight will deceive us. We have heard people say, "Seeing is believing." There's another variation of this saying used as colloquialism, "I'll believe it when I see it." This is not the attitude that we are encouraged by Paul to possess. Why? It is because Paul realized that what you see now doesn't necessarily determine what is going to take place.

Neither does it reflect what God is doing in the supernatural realm. Everything we see is temporary and subject to change.

Elisha, wearing the mantle of Elijah and operating in a double portion of his anointing, realized our sight will lie to us. The Bible tells us the story of a war between the Syrians and Israelites. It seemed as if Israel was always a step ahead of Syria and its king. Elisha was so keen and sharp in hearing from God that he knew where the Syrians would be camped before they even arrived at their destination.

The King of Syria was greatly troubled by this. He began to think that they had a spy within their ranks. When the King of Syria asked of his servants who is betraying him, they answered him this way, "None, my lord, O king; but Elisha, the prophet who is in Israel, tells the king of Israel the words that you speak in your bedroom" (2 Kings 6:12). So, the King of Syria found out Elisha was dwelling in Dothan and proceeded to send troops to retrieve him. What happened next was incredible.

> Therefore he sent horses and chariots and a great army there, and they came by night and surrounded the city. And when the servant of the man of God arose early and went out, there was an army, surrounding the city with horses and chariots. And his servant said to him, "Alas, my master! What shall we do?" So he answered, "Do not fear, for those who are with us are more than those who are with them." And Elisha prayed, and said, "Lord, I pray, open his eyes that he may see." Then the Lord opened the eyes of the young man, and he saw. And behold, the mountain was full of horses and chariots of fire all around Elisha (2 Kings 6:14-17).

God delivered a seemingly outnumbered prophet and his servant from the hand of the enemy. The servant was looking with the eyes of the flesh. There is something that is of greater reality than what we see with our eyes. David consistently referred to life as a shadow (Psalm 39:6, Psalm 102:11, Psalm 109:22) and this principle is stated by his son Solomon as well (Ecclesiastes 6:12, 8:13). A shadow is not the real thing and cannot harm you. Elisha's servant was in fear because of a shadow he was seeing. The servant failed to realize there were more for them than against them. Let me put it this way, what the servant saw lied to him.

Elisha had learned to look beyond what his eyes perceived and stood in faith. What enabled Elisha to have this confidence was knowing that God was for him. Know this: God is for you. You can have confidence that God will deliver you, regardless of what you may see right now.

I spent the first part of this chapter enumerating many issues that we are facing in our culture. Many believers in this day have allowed what they see to cause them to become discouraged and defeated. Therefore, it is so important that we walk by faith, not by what we see. Revolutionaries are not swayed by everything they see transpiring in the world. We stand fast knowing that Jesus has overcome the world. As revolutionaries, we don't live by what we see. We live by overcoming faith.

Have an Attitude of Victory

I'm a sports guy. Members in our congregation and anyone who knows me personally understands that I enjoy athletic competition. If you come into my home and the television is on, you are likely to find some sort of sporting event, sports recap show, or sports talk-show being broadcast. Whether it is basketball, mixed martial arts, professional football, boxing, hockey, or my favorite, college football (Go Noles), I love to watch sports.

One thing I have always pondered is what makes a team successful. Obviously, we understand that to be victorious one must be skilled. Moreover, one must have a successful game plan to attain victory. However, I believe there is another mental aspect that comes into play just as much as any physical attribute.

When one gets to the professional level, there is another aspect they must possess to see victory. In professional leagues, everyone is a phenomenal athlete. Many athletes are paid millions of dollars to play a game. They are all fantastic competitors. So, what separates the winners from the losers?

Paul "Bear" Bryant, coach of the University of Alabama football team from 1958-1982, during which period he won six national championships, said this, "If you believe in yourself and have dedication and pride—and never quit, you'll be a winner." I want to focus on what he said at the beginning of that quote, "If you believe…you'll be a winner." Let me put it this way. If you want to win you must have an attitude of victory that is rooted in faith: *a confident unshakeable expectation*. When he said to "believe in yourself," a large part of that is believing that you are destined for victory.

Solomon, the wisest man to ever live on this earth, backed up this ideology. In Proverbs 23:7 Solomon said this, "For as he thinks in his heart, so is he." We will become and manifest the fruit of what we think and believe about ourselves. People who are victorious in athletic competition have envisioned themselves as victors. In the minds of these combatants, winning is the only plausible outcome. I believe God desires for believers within the Church to increase the level of their faith.

Our Father in heaven wants us to be victorious. God designed and destined us for victory. He desires for His Church to walk in victory in this life. We must put the idea of defeat far from our minds. We can never embrace the lifestyle of being spiritual revolutionaries while we believe that we are destined for defeat. This ungodly mindset is a large part of the reason that we are experiencing the rise of ungodliness within our culture.

Believers have relinquished victory to the enemy rather than believing that God has a better glory and victory on the horizon for them. Many would rather forfeit than fight. Instead of entwining our identity with defeat, we must embrace a confident expectation. It is imperative we have faith that we are called to triumph. Just as Jesus was a winner, we are called to win. Let's look at the victory that Jesus accomplished for us and the triumph in which we are called to walk.

Jesus Victory Equals Your Victory

Jesus was the ultimate overcomer. He defeated death, hell, and the grave (Revelation 1:18). Just think about that for a moment. Is there any greater victory that you can imagine? Jesus was crucified and overcame death when He was resurrected on the third day. Not only did He defeat death, but in His resurrection He took the keys of hell and the grave. Our Savior didn't just defeat the enemy, He embarrassed him!

The Bible says this about the victory of Jesus and the show He made of the enemy: "He stripped all the spiritual tyrants in the universe of their sham authority at the Cross and marched them naked through the streets" (Colossians 2:15, MSG). I love that! Jesus didn't just defeat the enemy, He humiliated the enemy! Do you want to be like Jesus? Then understand you are called to victory. More than victory, you are also called to embarrass and humiliate the principalities and powers of darkness.

In John's Gospel, he gives an indicator of not only **how** to overcome the world, but he also identifies **who** will overcome the world. Who is it that will attain victory? It is the ones who are "born of God." Who are those who are born of God? That is an easy question to answer: BELIEVERS! 2 Corinthians 5:17 says, "Therefore, if anyone is in Christ, he is a new creation." If you belong to Christ, you have been born again. You are part of the "born of God" that John is referencing. That means that you are called to overcome the world.

Simon Peter said this:

> His divine power has given to us all things that pertain to life and godliness, through the knowledge of Him who called us by glory and virtue, by which have been given to us exceedingly great and precious promises, that through these you may be partakers of the divine nature (2 Peter 1:3-4).

I want to draw your attention to the fact that we have been made partakers. The word "partakers" is translated from the Greek word *koinōnós,* and it means *sharer.* As a born-again believer, you are a sharer of His victory. Those who are born of

God overcome the world. Why? It is because they share the same victory that Jesus accomplished.

Jesus was, is, and will always be the ultimate victor. We are called to be conformed to the image of the Son (Romans 8:29). We are predestined to be conformed to victory. We are fashioned for victory. Our destiny is victory. Why? It is because His destiny was victory. We are NOT helpless. We are victorious because we are the seed of Christ, the ultimate victor.

Seed will always produce after its own kind. I often have people tell me that I look like my father. More frequently, I have people share that they think I talk like my father. I hear most often that I have the mannerisms of my father. Why? It is because I am his seed. I really had no choice in the matter. It is part of my DNA because of the seed that created my life.

Jesus became the first-born among many brethren (Romans 8:29), and we are now part of the lineage—the seed of heaven. If Jesus walked in victory then we are to walk in victory. Why? It is because seed produces after its own kind. We have no choice if we are born-again—the seed of Christ. We will be victorious in Him. The victory that Jesus walked in means that we will walk in victory. Jesus' victory over the world equals our victory over the world.

Unrelenting Trust

I believe one of the greatest characteristics of overcoming faith is unrelenting trust. Those embracing the mantle of spiritual revolutionaries must possess this type of trust. Without unrelenting trust, we will ultimately falter and fail in our walk of faith. We must realize that what God is in the process of doing is not always what we see or experience in a season. That is why it is of great importance to have unrelenting and unflinching trust in God to work out all things for our good and ultimately for victory.

I believe there is no greater example in all of Scripture of unrelenting trust in God than Abram (Abraham). Let's look at the first recorded time that God spoke to him:

> Now the Lord had said to Abram: "Get out of your country, From your family And from your father's house, To a land that I will show you. I will make you a great nation; I will bless you And make your name great; And you shall be a blessing. I will bless those who bless you, And I will curse him who curses you; And in you all the families of the earth shall be blessed." So Abram departed as the Lord had spoken to him, and Lot went with him. And Abram was seventy-five years old when he departed from Haran (Genesis 12:1-4).

The very first time that God spoke to Abram He told him to leave everything that the man had ever known. There was no introduction, no build-up, just a command to go. You know that Abram had to have a firm conviction that He heard from God. Not only did Abram have to believe that he heard from God, he also had to believe that God would guide him. The Lord didn't give him a destination, just a command to go. Abram had to have unrelenting trust that God would perform His Word.

Of course, the bigger issue at play here is that God told Abram, "I will make you a great nation." In order to be a great nation Abram would need children. Abram was seventy-five years old. Now, I do not need to go into the details of biology to let you know that receiving this sort of promise at the golden age of 75 meant that God was going to have to do something miraculous. There is absolutely no inkling of evidence that Abram doubted that God was going to perform what He said. This is the reason Abram is such an incredible example of unrelenting faith. Nothing derailed him from believing what God had said.

Of course, most of us know the end of the story. Everything God promised Abraham came to fruition. Now, here is something that is key. It didn't happen without adversity, nor did it happen in the way Abraham necessarily imagined. However, in the end, God brought it to pass. Know this: it will not always be easy when you are walking out the manifestation of the promise. However, if you stay the course and stay in faith, you will see the promise fulfilled in your life and over this generation within the earth. Abraham saw the fulfillment God had for him. We will also see the fulfillment of what God has promised through prophets to do in the earth in this day if we will only trust Him. We, as revolutionaries, must simply live a lifestyle of unrelenting trust—a life of overcoming faith.

It Doesn't Take Much

We often keep ourselves from really standing in overcoming faith because we feel like we simply don't have enough faith. It doesn't take much faith to make a big difference. Jesus said, "I say to you, if you have faith as a mustard seed, you will say to this mountain, 'Move from here to there,' and it will move; and nothing will be impossible for you" (Matthew 17:20). Nothing will be impossible for us if we just have mustard seed faith.

Mustard seeds range between one to two millimeters in diameter. That is very small. Jesus said nothing will be impossible if you just have that size of faith. Far too often we fail to believe because we conclude we have insufficient faith. To be a spiritual revolutionary we must believe that our faith will work! The enemy wants to bind us and keep us from stepping out in faith. Why? It is because the devil realizes if we step out and believe what God said, it will spell bad news for him and for the systems of the world. If we will just have mustard seed-sized faith, we will turn the world upside down.

Overcoming faith is not about the size of your faith; it is about where your faith is placed. Understand this: your faith isn't in your ability to perform and turn the tide of what is going on in society. The greatest freedom you will ever know is that it is not your ability that brings about breakthrough. It is cooperating by faith with what Jesus has already done. My faith isn't in me; my faith is in Jesus. When we realize that by faith we are victorious and take that stand, we will see a change. Revolutionaries must possess and stand on overcoming faith. You will not be victorious one day; you are victorious now. Stand in overcoming faith and we will see the world turned upside down.

It is Time

I have faith in the revolutionaries God is raising up. We have reached a tipping point in time. The generation God is releasing in the earth is irrespective of age. The qualifier is the willingness to believe, lifting your voice, and marching in rank. Are you willing to join the ranks of the revolutionaries?

If we return back to the first chapter of this book and the dream that God gave me, there was a great company of people who were following the King of Kings as He marched toward the cityscape. These people were dressed in normal everyday clothing. As we close this book, I want you to envision yourself as part of that great company of people—that regiment of revolutionaries.

In the dream God gave me, there was an army marching in rank and order. See yourself as you march toward your school, your workplace, your house, or your church. Envision as you enter the place you've been called to effect and begin to release the Word of the Lord. You begin to prophesy destiny to the hurting and wandering. You begin to evangelize the lost and destitute. Those who are lost come to a realization of their identity as sons and daughters of the Most High God. Emptiness is filled in their lives as they begin to understand their purpose. Furthermore, you begin to minister to the needs of your family, and your entire household is saved. Your lost son, daughter, father, mother, niece, nephew, uncle, aunt, grandmother, grandfather—they are now fighting alongside you with their new identity as a revolutionary.

Continue to see yourself positioned in a strategic place to see the kingdom of God established in the earth. As you are faithful to stand and release what God has placed inside of you, suddenly, from the shadows, light will begin to break forth. The darkness that has hovered over your sphere of influence is broken as the Son comes shining down to destroy the evil work of the enemy. You look to your right, you look to your left, and you see that you are not alone. Surrounding you is a host of others now commissioned to be revolutionaries.

Do you believe you can see that happen? I believe it, and I believe you are called to see it become reality in your lifetime. I believe I am called to see it manifest in my lifetime.

The Revolutionaries are arising! Revolutionaries that will war! Revolutionaries that will contend! Revolutionaries that will prophesy! The time is now! The revolution now begins! REVOLUTIONARY, IT IS TIME TO CHANGE THE WORLD. TURN IT UPSIDE DOWN!

AFTERWORD

PASTOR ROBERT GAY
APOSTOLIC FOUNDER, HIGH PRAISE

Joshua Gay masterly and effectively communicates that God is releasing a revolutionary spirit within the Church today. His desire is to raise up revolutionaries that will go forth in the power of the Holy Spirit and see the kingdom of God established in the earth. Joshua has skillfully laid out principles that one needs working within their life to become one of God's revolutionaries. God has called all of us as members of the Church to turn the world upside down.

There are many things that are taking place in the earth today that need changing. It can clearly be seen that the world needs to change merely by watching any contemporary television program or sitcom. We observe the promotion of wrong and sinful things as we are told these things are right and virtuous. We see the proliferation of things that would even be repulsive to unbelievers fifty years ago. We are in an age where wrong is being praised as right, and right is being condemned as being wrong. We need a spiritual revolution!

Throughout the history of mankind, God has always sought for a man to work through. Ezekiel declared that God "sought for a man among them who would make a wall" (Ezekiel 22:30).

Unfortunately, he went on to say that God could not find anyone. I believe that Jesus is the same yesterday, today, and forever. He is still looking and seeking for those who are willing to become the ones to enforce change in the earth.

Anytime that God found a man willing to be used by Him, great and powerful things happened. Men like Abraham, Joseph, Moses, David, Elijah, Daniel, and Paul brought change to the culture of their day. They were change-makers. They were dissatisfied with the status-quo and allowed themselves to be used by the Spirit of the Lord to enact transformation. Likewise, God is looking for men and women today who are willing to be used as kingdom enforcers.

We have a choice today. We can sit back and take the attitude of the 10 spies who said, "We are not able." We can sit back and say we are nothing but "grasshoppers," and the giants are so much bigger and mightier. Or, we can be like Joshua and Caleb and declare, "We are able!" We can respond to the call of God to be a revolutionary and allow His Spirit to work mightily within us to enact and enforce the rule of the kingdom of God in the earth. The choice is ours.

As for me and my house, we have made our decision. We have made our decision to be agents of revolution. We have made our decision to be giant killers. We have made our decision to arise, face the challenge, and overcome! We can all do this together by the power of the Holy Spirit if we will just say, "YES!" We only need to correctly respond to the call of God today. We can and we will by His grace and power.

In the Bible, we read the account of four lepers who were at the entrance of the gate of the city (2 Kings 7:1-3). When surrounded by a walled city on one side, the enemy on the other side, and famine throughout the land, they said, "Why sit here until we die?" Likewise, the Church at large has been figuratively standing at the gate. However, it is time for action! No longer is there time for standing around while staring at the gate. Don't procrastinate and wait for another season. Heaven needs you now! Now is the time and this is the day. Enlist yourself in the army of the Lord and become one of His revolutionaries.

Come on....LET'S DO THIS!

BIBLIOGRAPHY

Chapter 2, Pages 14-15 – Washington's letter
"General Orders, 2 July 1776," Founders Online, National Archives, last modified February 21, 2017. http://founders.archives.gov/documents/Washington/03-05-02-0117. [Original source: The Papers of George Washington, Revolutionary War Series, vol. 5, 16 June 1776–12 August 1776, ed. Philander D. Chase. Charlottesville: University Press of Virginia, 1993, pp. 179–182].

Chapter 2, Page 17 – Lord North quote
Eccleston, Jim. "Chronology of Events After The Siege." National Parks Service. 1993. Accessed March 20, 2017. https://www.nps.gov/york/learn/historyculture/afterthesiege.htm.

Chapter 2, Page 21 – Revolutionary definition
"Revolutionary." Merriam-Webster. Accessed March 20, 2017. https://www.merriam-webster.com/dictionary/revolutionary.

Chapter 2, Page 21 – Revolution Definition
"Revolution." Merriam-Webster. Accessed March 20, 2017. https://www.merriam-webster.com/dictionary/revolution.

Chapter 3, Pages 37-38 – Adams letter
"From John Adams to Hezekiah Niles, 13 February 1818," Founders Online, National Archives, last modified December 28, 2016. http://founders.archives.gov/documents/Adams/99-02-02-6854.

Chapter 3, Page 39 – Serle Quote
Great Britain. ***The Manuscripts of the Earl of Dartmouth.*** London, Printed for H.M. Stationery Office, by Eyre and Spottiswoode, 1887. 427.

Chapter 3, Page 39 – Presbyterian Ministers and the Revolution
Baldwin, Alice M., and University of Connecticut Libraries. ***The New England Clergy and the American Revolution***. Durham, North Carolina: Duke University Press, 1928.

Chapter 3, Page 40 – King George III "Presbyterian War"
Douglas F. Kelly, ***The Emergence of Liberty in the Modern World: The Influence of Calvin on Five Governments from the 16th Through 18th Centuries***. Philipsburg, N.J.: P&R Publishing, 1992. 131.

Chapter 3, Page 40 – Students are full of God quote
The Calcutta Christian Observer. Vol. 8. (1839) 425.

Chapter 3, Page 42 – Franklin Letter
Franklin, Benjamin, and Charles William Elliot. ***The Autobiography of Benjamin Franklin***. 2012. Kindle. 100.

Chapter 3, Page 43 - William Perry quote
Hyatt, Eddie L. ***Pilgrims and Patriots: The Radical Christian Roots of American Democracy and Freedom***. Grapevine, TX: Hyatt Press, 2016. 108.

Chapter 4, Page 44 – Moody Quote
Fackler, Mark. "The World Has Yet to See..." Christianitytoday.com. Accessed March 20, 2017. http://www.christianitytoday.com/history/issues/issue-25/world-has-yet-to-see.html.

Chapter 4, Page 44 – Consecrated Definition
"Consecrated" Merriam-Webster. Accessed March 20, 2017. https://www.merriam-webster.com/dictionary/consecrated.

Chapter 4, Page 52-53 – "Send The Fire" lyrics
"Songs of Love and Praise No. 2 for Use in Meetings for Christian Worship or Work." P. 160. Hymnary.org. Accessed March 20, 2017. http://www.hymnary.org/hymn/SLP21895/page/160.

Chapter 5, Page 63 – University of Bristol Study
Koutsikou, Stella, Jonathan J. Crook, Emma V. Earl, J. Lianne Leith, Thomas C. Watson, Bridget M. Lumb, and Richard Apps. "Neural Substrates Underlying Fear-evoked Freezing: The Periaqueductal Greycerebellar Link." The Journal of Physiology 592, no. 10 (2014): 2197-213. doi:10.1113/jphysiol.2013.268714.

Chapter 5, Page 70 – Roosevelt Quote
"A Quote by Theodore Roosevelt." Goodreads. Accessed March 20, 2017. http://www.goodreads.com/quotes/312751-nothing-in-the-world-is-worth-having-or-worth-doing.

Chapter 6, Pages 71-72 – Churchill Quote
Olsen, John. "We Shall Fight on the Beaches." The Churchill Centre. Accessed March 20, 2017. http://www.winstonchurchill.org/resources/speeches/1940-the-finest-hour/128-we-shall-fight-on-the-beaches.

Chapter 6, Page 87, The American Crisi
Paine, Thomas. "The American Crisis (No. 1) By the Author of Common Sense. [Boston] Sold opposite the Court House Queen Street [1776]." The Library of Congress. Accessed March 20, 2017. https://www.loc.gov/item/rbpe.03902300/.

Chapter 7, Page 106 – Plesion Definition
"Mark Chapter 12 (KJV)." Blue Letter Bible. Accessed March 20, 2017. https://www.blueletterbible.org/lang/lexicon/lexicon.cfm?Strongs=G4139&t=NKJV.

Chapter 7, Page 107 – Mayflower Compact
"Avalon Project - Mayflower Compact: 1620." Avalon.law.yale.edu. Accessed March 20, 2017. http://avalon.law.yale.edu/17th_century/mayflower.asp.

Chapter 9, Page 135 – Loyalists Percentages
Green, Jack P., and J. R. Pole. "A Companion to the American Revolution." A Companion to the American Revolution, 2003, 235-47. Accessed March 21, 2017. doi:10.1111/b.9781405116749.2003.00032.x.

Chapter 10, Page 139 – Millennial Statistics
Liu, Joseph. "Religion Among the Millennials." Pew Research Center's Religion & Public Life Project. February 16, 2010. Accessed March 21, 2017. http://www.pewforum.org/2010/02/17/religion-among-the-millennials/.

Chapter 10, Page 144 – Bear Bryant Quote
Roberts, Drew. "10 Bear Bryant Quotes For Alabama Fans On 10/10/10." Saturday Down South. October 10, 2010. Accessed March 21, 2017. https://www.saturdaydownsouth.com/2010/paul-bear-bryant-quotes-for-alabama-fans/.

ABOUT THE AUTHOR

Joshua Gay is the lead pastor of High Praise in Orlando, Florida. He began serving in ministry at a young age and has dedicated his life to promoting and propagating the Gospel of Jesus Christ. Joshua's zeal for the Word and his passion for the presence of God have touched the hearts of those both young and old. His teachings are illuminating and revelatory bringing encouragement to all who hear them. *For complete bio go to www.highpraiseorlando.com.*

CONNECT WITH JOSHUA GAY

FACEBOOK.COM/PASTORJOSHUAGAY TWITTER.COM/PASTORJOSHUAGAY

for more information on available products or ministry scheduling, contact us at: highpraiseorlando.com

HIGHPRAISE

ONLINE

VISIT US ONLINE TODAY!

highpraisepc.com

highpraiseorlando.com

HIGHPRAISE
ORLANDO
SUN: 10:00AM // WED: 7:15PM
CONNECT WITH US ONLINE @HIGHPRAISEORLANDO
Instagram
HIGHPRAISEORLANDO.COM
SCAN HERE FOR
MORE INFO ABOUT
HIGH PRAISE
ORLANDO
pastors
JOSHUA & MIRANDA GAY

HIGHPRAISE
PODCAST
Search 'High Praise' in iTunes
subscribe and listen to many powerful messages by
Pastor Joshua Gay, Apostle Robert Gay & more
SCAN QR CODE TO GO TO
HIGH PRAISE
PODCASTS

HIGH PRAISE MEDIA

PRODUCTS

Next Level: Raising The Standard Of Grace

Pastor Robert Gay

In this book, Robert is sounding a trumpet call from heaven, engaging the reader to see the Ten Commandments afresh from the empowering view of God's Grace. Robert clearly and biblically explains how Grace takes the Ten Commandments to the *Next Level* and empowers us to live godly, holy lives above sin. There is no limit to the success, prosperity & blessings that will surround you when you apply the principles of *Next Level.*

Conquering King

High Praise Worship

This album is packed full of powerful and anointed praise and worship that will usher you into the presence of the Lord. This album features songs such as: *God Is Fighting, I Believe, Great Is The Lord, Awesome God, I Will Worship, Jehovah Jireh, Mercy Rain, We Are Overcomers, Conquering King* and more.

for more info or to order any of these porducts visit our online store at

WWW.HIGHPRAISEPC.COM/ONLINE-STORE

Silencing The Enemy With Praise

Pastor Robert Gay

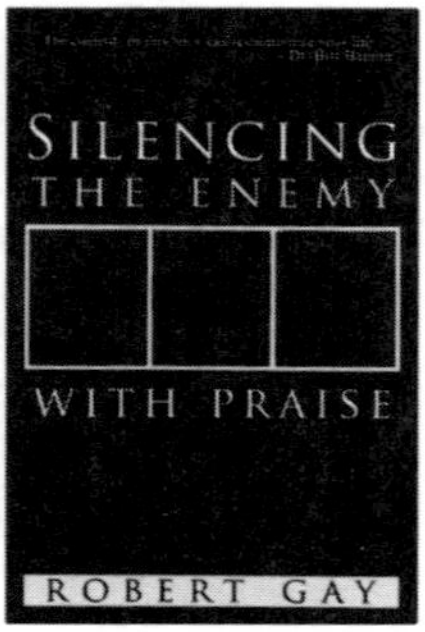

Praise and worship are more than words and music says author Pastor Robert Gay. Praise is a weapon of warfare. God will fight for you as you praise the greatness of His name.

"The contents of this book can revolutionize your life...It brings new understanding about the power of praise and worship."
-Dr. Bill Hamon

Planted

Pastor Robert Gay

Robert Gay confronts common "church issues" head on. He teaches with clarity and compassion that God is the Master Gardener who lovengly tends to every individual planted in His garden. You will find out how God wants to plant you so that you will flourish and grow and become everything He wants you to be.

"Every Pastor will appreciate this book...every saint of God should read this book..." - Dr. Bill Hamon

Best Of Robert Gay

Pastor Robert Gay

This compilation album represents some of Robert's most impactful songs that have touched the body of Christ throughout the world. This cd is packed full with 19 tracks that include powerful songs such as Mighty Man of War, Lord Sabaoth, On Bended Knee, Holy is Your Name, One Voice, No Other Name and much more!

HIGH PRAISE MEDIA PRODUCTS **for more products or to order any of these porducts visit our online store at WWW.HIGHPRAISEPC.COM/ONLINE-STORE**

Sonship
Pastor Joshua Gay

Discover the life of a true son through study of the Scripture and powerful testimonies. The author shines the light on many pitfalls that ensnare today's generation while revealing the true picture of faithful spiritual sons and daughters.

"This book needs to be read by every person who wants to be a true son or father according to God's order." - Dr. Bill Hamon

Faith Force Academy LIVE DVD
Volume 1: Meet The Faith Force

Join the Faith Force Heroes and Professors M & C in *Faith Force Academy LIVE!* as they teach you how to become strong superheroes of faith! This volume contains 4 exciting episodes that kids of all ages will be sure to enjoy. Each episode features exciting praise & worship, step by step teaching of scripture memory verses, incredible life-sized characters, & illustrated sermons.

Faith Force Academy LIVE DVD
Volume 2: Faith Is The Victory

Join the Faith Force Heroes and Professors M & C in *Faith Force Academy LIVE!* as they teach you how faith is our victory! This volume contains 4 exciting episodes that kids of all ages will be sure to enjoy. Each episode features exciting praise & worship, step by step teaching of scripture memory verses, incredible life-sized characters, & illustrated sermons.

HIGH PRAISE MEDIA PRODUCTS for more products or to order any of these products visit our online store at WWW.HIGHPRAISEPC.COM/ONLINE-STORE

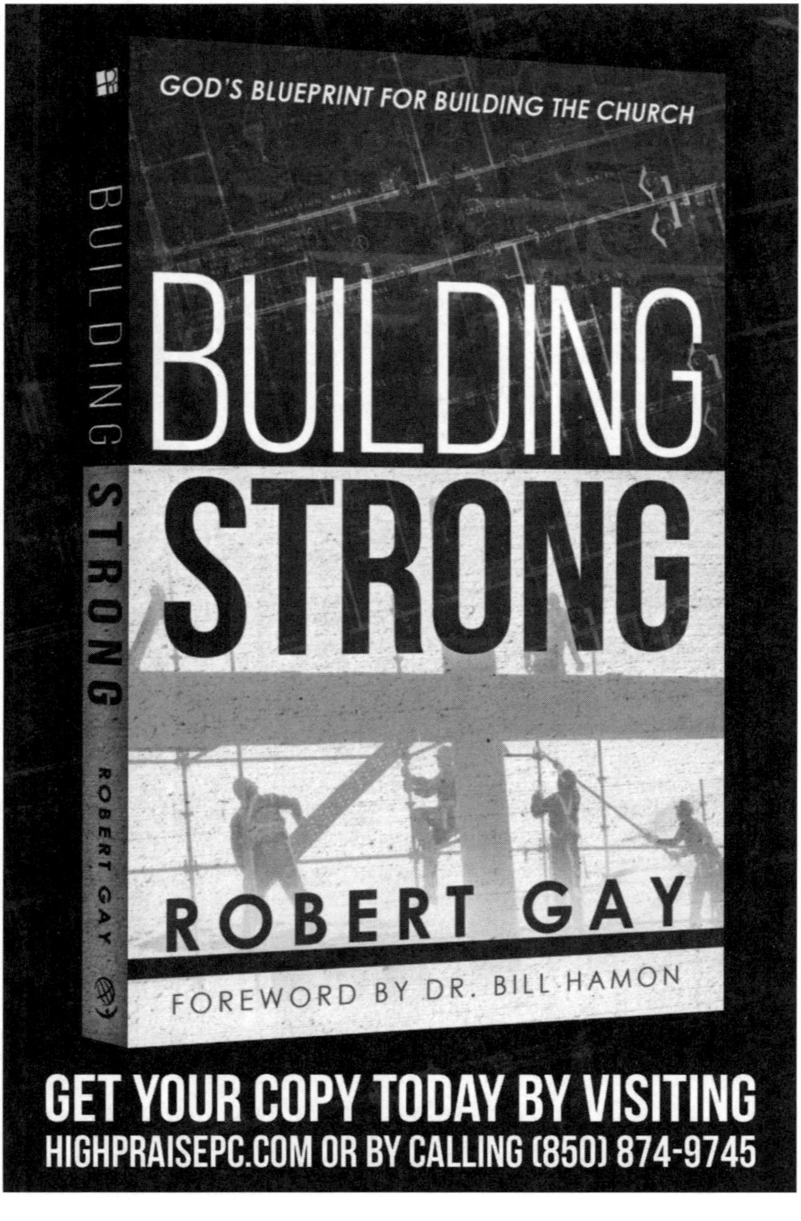
GOD'S BLUEPRINT FOR BUILDING THE CHURCH
BUILDING
STRONG
ROBERT GAY
FOREWORD BY DR. BILL HAMON
BUILDING STRONG
ROBERT GAY
GET YOUR COPY TODAY BY VISITING
HIGHPRAISEPC.COM OR BY CALLING (850) 874-9745

HIGHPRAISE
PANAMA CITY
SUN: 9AM & 11AM // WED: 7PM
CONNECT WITH US ONLINE @HIGHPRAISEPC
Instagram
HIGHPRAISEPC.COM
SCAN HERE FOR
MORE INFO ABOUT
HIGH PRAISE
PANAMA CITY
pastors
ROBERT & STACEY GAY

GET SOCIAL WITH US

@HIGHPRAISEPC
@HIGHPRAISEORL

Parsons Publishing House

Your Voice Your World™

NEXT LEVEL

Raising the Standard of Grace

by Pastor Robert Gay

ISBN: 9781602730427 • 216 pages • $14.95 USD.

CAPTURING THE HEART OF GOD

Pleasing the Father in Everyday Life

by Diane Parsons

ISBN: 9781602730082 • 128 pages • $10.95 USD.

OUT OF BALANCE INTO RHYTHM

Finding Joy and Peace as You Live Life with God

by Frank Maycock

ISBN: 9781602730786 • 192 pages • $14.95 USD.

SETTING THE COURSE FOR FUTURE GENERATIONS

by Shane Huseby

ISBN: 9781602730243 • 120 pages • $9.95 USD.

SURVIVING THE CHALLENGES OF TRANSITION

by Dr. Gerald Doggett

ISBN: 9781602730182 • 140 pages • $12.95 USD.

Parsons Publishing House

Your Voice Your World™

EMERGING AS AN INNOVATIVE CHRISTIAN LEADER

by Dr. Darrell Parsons

ISBN: 9781602730656 • 228 pages • $14.95 USD.

JESUS IN 3D

Living in the Fullness of God

by Pastor Robert Gay

ISBN: 9781602730588 • 102 pages• $9.95 USD.

BUILDING STRONG

God's Blueprint for Building the Church

by Pastor Robert Gay

ISBN: 9781602730892 • 224 pages • $14.95 USD.

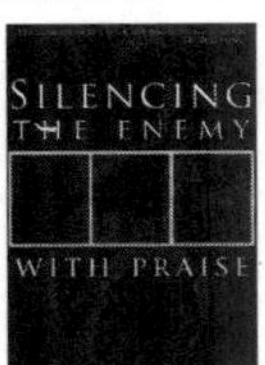

SILENCING THE ENEMY WITH PRAISE

by Pastor Robert Gay

ISBN: 9781602730052 • 156 pages • $11.95 USD.

SONSHIP

The Mantle. The Journey. The Double Portion.

by Pastor Joshua Gay

ISBN: 9781602730526 • 180 pages • $12.95 USD.

Parsons Publishing House

Your Voice Your World™

70 REASONS FOR SPEAKING IN TONGUES
Your Own Built in Spiritual Dynamo
by Dr. Bill Hamon
ISBN: 9781602730137 • 216 pages • $14.95 USD.

UPRIGHTING RELATIONSHIPS
by Linda Roeder
ISBN: 9781602730755 • 174 pages • $12.95 USD.

FAITH AFTER FAILURE
Reconnecting with Your Destiny
by Sandie Freed
ISBN: 9781602730557 • 208 pages • $13.95 USD.

WHY DO I DO THE THINGS I DO?
Understanding Personalities
by Dr. Darrell Parsons
ISBN: 9781602730199 • 132 pages • $10.95 USD.

**RELEASE YOUR WORDS—
IMPACT YOUR WORLD**
by Dr. Darrell Parsons
ISBN: 9781602730007 • 140 pages • $9.95 USD.